C0-EDW-992

NORTH COUNTRY BASSIN'

by
Tom Zenanko

Artwork by Buzz Buczynski, Brookston, Minn.
Cover and Inside Photos by Author

Tom Zenanko Outdoors

ISBN 0-9610296-2-5
Library of Congress Number 84-90656
Copyright© 1984 by Tom Zenanko Outdoors
All Rights Reserved

NORTH COUNTRY BASSIN'

TABLE OF CONTENTS

1. The World of the Bass 3

2. Seasonal Bass Movements in Lakes and Rivers 9
   Largemouth Fishing Through the Seasons
   Seasonal Movements of Smallmouth

3. Shallow Water Bassin' Tactics 37
   Topwater Fishing Tricks
   The Art of Spinnerbaiting
   Spoon Fishing for Bass

4. In-Between Tactics for Bass Fishing 75
   Bass on Crankbaits
   Plastic Worm Fishing

5. Deep Water Bassin' 93

6. Bassin' Rods and Reels 100
   Fishing Lines and Knots

7. Boats for Bass Fishing 115
   Bass Fishing Accessories
   Electronics

8. Specialized Bassin' Tactics 136
   Boat Dock Bass
   Bog Bass Fishing
   Fishing the Slop for Largemouth
   Bass in Reeds
   River Smallmouth Tactics

9. Weather Affects on Bass 172
10. Tournament Fishing Strategies 177
    Team or Individual Competition
11. Fishing a New Lake 191
12. Fly Fishing for Bass 194
13. Live Bait for Bass 202
14. State and World Bass Records 211

This book is dedicated to my parents who realized I would never be a doctor, so they let me go fishing. A special thanks to my friends and neighbors, a group of great folks who really made this book possible.

INTRODUCTION

In recent years, there has been a boom in the popularity of bass fishing. This boom has been part of a major change in the thinking of many fishermen all across the country. This book is one of many on the subject of bass fishing, but it is very special. This bass book deals with the strategies, methods, and styles of fishing bass in Yankee country.

The major boom in bass fishing has been greatly influenced by the states below the Mason Dixon line. Big money contests, world bass fishing championships, and the formation of bass fishing clubs all added to the excitement over bass fishing. Here, in the northern regions of the United States, the popularity of bass fishing is still quite small compared to the number of anglers who are in search of walleyes.

It is not that anglers here in the north do not appreciate the challenge and sport of catching largemouth and smallmouth bass. Thousands of anglers in the upper regions of the United States participate in bass fishing tournaments and belong to bass fishing organizations. There is such a variety of great fishing found in our natural lakes region of the country that bass fishing doesn't get much exposure. NORTH COUNTRY BASSIN' is the first book ever dedicated exclusively to the largemouth and smallmouth bass fishing in the natural lakes in the northern regions of our great country. Now, more than ever, anglers will need to know the methods and techniques for catching bass close to home, bringing pride in the quality of fishing we have.

In surveys conducted at my various fishing seminars, one obvious fact about the interests of the fishermen in the North Country kept shining through. A big majority of the anglers still go fishing to fill their freezers! This fact may sound rather cruel, but it is true. There has been a big trend towards fishing more for sport than for food. Organizations like Muskies Inc., Trout Unlimited, Minnesota

Northern Pike Association, Walleyes Unlimited and sport fishing federations are gaining momentum very quickly.

The largemouth bass is truly a sportfish, and in my fishing seminars I often refer to these great fish as the "sportfish of the 80's". This phrase covers the feeling I have as an angler towards these great fish. Not only are they a challenging adversary, who can test your wit and skills to the limit, but they also can be released after a battle to be caught again and again.

Because there are so many aspects of bass fishing to cover, it is hard to do it all. At first, my problem was to not make this book too large or too complicated. My two other best selling books called **WALLEYE FISHING TODAY** and **NORTHERN PIKE!** did this very well. In the fishing tackle business today, there is a lot of hype about this product or that method of fishing. Anglers tend to get a distorted view of the things they really need to know to be a successful fisherman. **NORTH COUNTRY BASSIN'** promises to be clear and direct.

The bass is a true sport fish and it is my hope that more anglers in the North Country and elsewhere in the country realize its importance. In this book, there are hundreds of facts and tips about bass fishing today, but never forget that fishing is fun too!

CHAPTER ONE

THE WORLD OF THE BASS

The bass is a member of the sunfish family. In the United States are there eight different species of bass and many more species of sunfish. Here in the North Country, we have just two species of bass, the largemouth and smallmouth bass. Even though these two fish are of the same species, these fish are different in many ways.

From a fisherman's point of view, it is a good idea to know the differences in bass behavior. The brain of a bass is about the size of a pea. Bass, like all fish, simply respond to their environment. The more we, the fishermen, can think like a fish, the easier it will become to locate the fish. Unfortunately, there are countless variables which can affect bass movements. No book has ever been written to cover all the possible variations. The only way this could be done would be to a book on each and every lake that holds a bass.

Largemouth Bass, Micropterus Salmoides

The natural range of the largemouth bass covers most of the United States east of the Rockies. It is not known exactly how bass got into some isolated lakes in southern Canada. The largemouth has proven to be very adaptable to all sorts of water conditions.

It is commonly accepted that there are different "strains" of bass in the United States. The Florida strain is capable of growing very large in a short period of time. Here in the north, it is believed that the Florida strain would not be able to survive our cold winters.

The world record bass is 22 pounds, 4 ounces taken from Lake Montgomery in 1932. A trophy largemouth bass in the north is anything over five pounds, but seven pounders are real braggin' size.

Being able to identify a largemouth from a smallmouth is not all that difficult. If you are unable to notice the obviously large mouth and faint lateral line found with a largemouth, there are more scientific ways of checking it out. If you were to draw a line straight down from the back of the eye on a largemouth, the lower jaw would extend beyond the line. There are often nine hard spines and 12 or 13 soft rays in the dorsal fin with a sharp groove separating the two dorsal fins.

Young largemouth bass are almost transparent in color with a very distinct lateral line running along the sides. As they grow, this line becomes less and less visible.

The largemouth in our North Country often range in color from a very dark green to an almost pale silver color. These changes in body color seem to reflect the kind of water the fish live in. The bass from a gin clear lake have very white bellies and dark green backs, while bass from a heavily silted lake are very pale and look washed out. No matter what their shade of color, they are still 100% pure bass.

The hatchery rearing of bass has not worked out very well at all. The best method for obtaining fry is to place several adult fish in a small pond and let them do their own thing. Bass spawn when water temperatures reach the mid sixties. They prefer the protected areas of a lake which are often along the northern shores. The northern shores receive more springtime sun and warm up many times faster than the rest of the lake.

The male bass does all the work during the spawning season. They fin out a sandy depression in the bottom about three feet in diameter. These male bass are very territorial and will not place a nest within ten feet of another bass. When the female comes onto the nest and lays the eggs, the male fertilizes them and she is off. From that point on the male protects the nest from any intruders, large or small. Although the male bass never grows as large as the females, they make up for their size with toughness. All the while they are on the nests, the male bass will not feed at all!

The male protects the eggs until they hatch and the young have reached about one inch in length. From that point on, if the fry don't find cover to hide in, they will end up being devoured by Dad! In a controlled pond situation, 4,000 fry can be expected out of each nest. In a natural setting, it is very important that mother nature be kind to the eggs before they hatch. A strong wind shift could wash the eggs ashore. A sudden drop in temperature will force the male bass to abandon the nest and the eggs will fall prey to hungry panfish nearby. Even if silt covers the eggs, the male bass will leave the nest thinking all is lost.

Adult bass will feed on anything they can grab, from black birds to snakes. One of the reasons for their great adaptability is their willingness to feed on anything they can get their mouths around! Both largemouth and smallmouth bass feed very little during the winter months. For all practical purposes, they become totally inactive through the winter, they don't grow, they don't eat, they don't move. Only on rare occasions do ice fishermen get a chance to hook a bass through the ice.

Smallmouth Bass, Micropterus Dolomieui

The original range of the smallmouth bass was located in the upper regions of the Mississippi River system, the St. Lawrence River system, the Great Lakes (except Lake Superior), and much of the middle and northeastern United States. The smallmouth is a very special fish in that it is the tough kid on the block in lakes where it lives. A very bold fish for its size, the smallmouth is not nearly as tough as bass lovers would like to believe. Extensive stocking programs have brought success in some areas and failure in others. In many ways, the early stocking programs were a hit and miss operation. At the turn of the century, bass were transported by train in large milk cans and released in any waters in which it was thought the bass would survive.

Know The Difference:

- Joined dorsal fins
- Some scales present
- imaginary vertical line
- Vertical line just nicks upper jaw

SMALLMOUTH BASS

- almost separated
- no scales present
- upper jaw well past vertical line

LARGEMOUTH BASS

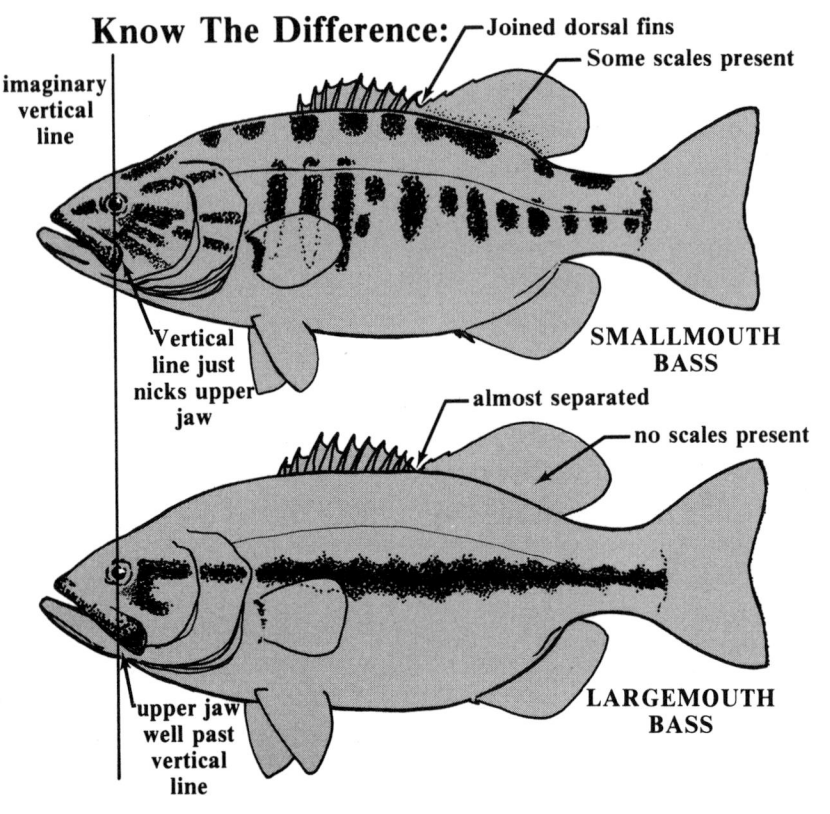

In some areas it was a great success, in others it was a complete failure. Some of the finest smallmouth fishing in America today is located along the Canadian border, and it has all come about through stocking programs.

The world record smallmouth is 11 pounds, 15 ounces taken from Dale Hollow Lake in Kentucky by David Hayes in 1955. Here in the North Country a four pounder is a great fish, and several in the six pound range are taken every year.

The coloration of an adult smallmouth ranges from a pale green to a very dark brown. Many refer to the smallmouth as a "bronzeback" because its sides are often a rich bronze-like color. Although the largemouth seems to change color patterns with the water in which it lives, I have not seen this trend with smallmouth. Several times I have fished an area taking "green" and "brown" smallmouth with equal frequency.

Young fry are always very dark or totally black in color. They are much different than the almost transparent fry of the largemouth. As they mature, the color markings often resemble vertical bars. The older the bass, the less pronounced the bars will be.

Many anglers have a hard time telling the difference between a small largemouth and a smallmouth. To identify the smallmouth, the lower jaw will not extend beyond the eye. Also, the dorsal fin can have 9 spines like a largemouth, but it has 13 to 15 soft spines. The two dorsal fins are lower than the largemouth's and do not have a pronounced break between them. The absence of the dark lateral line is one of the big tip offs, plus the substantially smaller jaw.

The smallmouth spawns slightly later in the year than the largemouth. The nest of the smallie is also tended to by the male. Their nests are not nearly as fancy as a largemouth's, and they prefer to dig out a small area around some object such as a rock or fallen log. The smallmouth also likes protected bays, often with sand or small rocks on the bottom. Unlike the largemouth, if the smallmouth finds conditions bad for spawning, they postpone their activity and try again later in the year. It is very possible to find smallmouth on nests as late as August!

Smallmouth bass simply love crayfish. Any lake which plans on having a natural supply of smallmouth had better have plenty of crayfish to go around. The smallie has also learned to take advantage of small fishes when they are abundant in a lake or river. Where a largemouth might prefer weedy areas on a lake or river system, the smallmouth prefers cleaner bottom areas with current or wave action if possible.

Smallmouth prefer to build nests around objects along the bottom. The male smallmouth is also the smaller of the two and is the one who protects the nest until the fry leave the nest. A male bass will readily strike a lure that passes near a nest, but does so to protect the nest, not to feed.

CHAPTER TWO

SEASONAL BASS MOVEMENTS IN LAKES AND RIVERS

Understanding daily and seasonal movements of bass is a complex problem. Predicting how and why bass move is risky business for the outdoor writer. A blanket statement about ALL bass is never 100% correct. Exceptions to every rule can be found once you have spent a little time on your favorite bassin' hole.

On the other hand, many anglers believe a lake in Wisconsin has little in common with a lake in New York. From a fishing standpoint, the lakes could be identical in how they should be fished. The big difference in this book over others on bass fishing is NOT the fish itself. A bass is a bass is a bass, no matter where it lives. The key difference is how it reacts to the changes in seasons and the different types of habitat found in the natural lakes of the North Country.

As fishermen, every day we spend on the water will bring a new awareness to the movements and habits of bass. Three major factors will control how and why bass move. They are FOOD, SECURITY, and COMFORT. In the back of every fisherman's mind, these three factors will be the cornerstone for finding fish no matter where you fish. In this section we will cover largemouth bass in lakes first, then move to the smallmouth in lakes and rivers.

Wintering Largemouth Habits

Rather than beginning with the seasonal changes starting in the spring, I felt it better to start when the bass are least active. Water temperature is one of the major factors which controls bass activity. Of all freshwater fishes, the largemouth and smallmouth bass are affected the most by cold water temperatures. Anglers must be aware of this if they ever hope to find and catch bass consistently.

When ice is covering our lakes, the bass are tightly schooled in small pockets just outside the first major drop-off of the lake. In the backwaters of the lower Mississippi, bass seek out deep pockets with no current flow at all, if possible. Hundreds of bass can be found in a small depression in an otherwise shallow river bottom.

The best way to describe what happens to bass during the winter is that they simply go to sleep. They feed very little, if at all, and move only a few yards over a four month period. The bass are not going to starve just because they don't eat. The metabolism of bass is slowed to the point that they require little food. In this cold water period, bass will not grow.

In the cooling ponds of power plants in states such as North Dakota, the bass do very well. These ponds have been stocked with bass and other panfish. The waters are kept open and warm all year long. In this unique situation, the bass grow and feed all year long and some real hawgs have been caught. Although the air temperature may be ten degrees below zero, many of these lakes have a water temperature in the sixties. Anglers can use spring and mid-summer tactics to catch bass all winter long!

In natural lakes, catching a bass through the ice is more an exception than a rule. You may read stories of fishermen catching bass early in the season, but going out to actually catch a bass through the ice is almost an impossible task. Face it, any fish that doesn't move, eat, or grow under the ice will be hard to catch by any legal means.

Ice-Out Largemouth

In many North Country states, there are laws regulating the seasons for bass fishing. This is done to protect spawning brood stock from being taken when they are in heavy concentrations. Depending on the state in which you live, the seasons may vary a great deal. Biologists don't agree on exactly what is best for bass management in the north.

I do not encourage any of my readers to violate the laws of their state. Certain sections of this chapter will naturally be useless to anglers living in states with a closed season on bass, especially right after ice out. In some states, catching bass before the season opens can be grounds for fish harassment charges. Please check to find out what the laws are in your area before you start catching bass.

As the ice leaves our northern lakes, bass activity is slow to almost non-existent. Water temperatures in the low 40's still restrict bass movement a great deal. Only on rare occasions will anglers be able to see any action from these bass unless very small forms of live bait are used, like crappie minnows or very small jigs.

It doesn't take long for the spring sun to warm up portions of the lake to draw up the bass. Since cold water slows down bass activity, any increase in water temperature is good. Wintering bass hold in deep water while ice covers the lakes, but the urge to spawn motivates them to seek out warmer waters and ripen the eggs they carry.

Many of the first areas bass move into in early spring are the same as where the crappie fishermen hang out. Many a crappie angler has taken a trophy bass while fishing at this time of year on light tackle. The bass are there to feed, and although many of the bass are females in the two to four pound range, the best lures are still the small crappie jigs.

As water temperatures increase, so does the activity level of the bass. In tight schools, bass feed on small panfish and minnows which are also drawn to the warmest waters of a lake. These areas could include private boat channels or shallow protected bays that are often too weedy during the season for you to fish. A muck bottom is far better for finding bass at this time of year simply because it warms quickly under sunlight.

Even kids can enjoy the thrill of catching a nice bass and learn young in life the importance of catch and release fishing. There is no better thrill for parents than to see their children land their first bass and to have them want to put it back.

If a cold spell settles in, the bass simply move back out into slightly deeper water where the water temperatures are more constant. The time of day for peak bass activity is also temperature related. If the water is cold in the morning, activity of the bass will peak about mid-day after the water has warmed up.

The warmer the water gets, the more aggressive the bass becomes. This time of year is known as the pre-spawn period. Bass anglers love this time of year. Large schools of bass are concentrated in the shallows, and in some shallow protected bays every cast will see action. We North Country anglers can expect this pre-spawn activity to take place anytime between April 15 and May 20 on an average spring.

Spawning Bass Habits

As we approach the end of May, bass will start moving into areas to spawn. The male bass move into shallow protected bays that have a sandy bottom base. A layer of muck may cover the bottom, but, the male bass brushes the area clean with his tail and builds a nest.

At this time of year the lilac bushes are just beginning to bloom. The large egg-carrying females wait in deeper water just off the nesting areas for their time. Anglers can often catch the largest bass of the year just before the bass move up to the nests. The females do feed at this time, in contrast to the males who do not eat until the spawning cycle is complete.

Anglers can often spot these nests along shore if they move their boats quietly along the shore. The male bass will hit almost any lure to chase it out of the nest. People may think that the bass are hungry because they hit anything that moves, but the true fact of the matter is that they strike to protect the nest only and don't plan on eating a thing.

Catching a bass off a nest is not often a wise idea. The female bass comes in and lays her eggs, but quickly leaves to let the male carry out his duties. If any other fish or creature tries to get at the eggs, the male bass fights to his death to scare it off. If the bass is taken off the nest for too long a period, a school of sunfish could easily clean the nest out. Fishing bass on beds is great sport, but it may create problems for future bass populations in this body of water.

Early Summer Bassin'

The spawning cycle is often complete by the first week of June through most of the north. There is a transition period for bass as they come out of their spawning cycle that could make it tough for the fisherman. Not all bass will be spawning at the same time and this means that not all bass will be ready to start feeding again at the same time. If the spawning area is located in a fairly large bay or a shallow flat area, the bass may stay in the area for quite a while. Spawning areas that have large reed banks often hold post-spawn bass for several weeks.

As each bass stops spawning at its own pace, the groups of bass begin to get larger and larger on what is called the inside edges of weed lines. For example; weeds in a lake have yet to grow to the surface, but you can see that some are just starting, the best bass action will not be found on the outside of the weed edge, but on the inside edge next to shore.

There is a steady progression in bass movements as spring turns to summer. The major groupings of bass move from the inside edge to the outside edge of the weeds on a lake. The weed growth on a lake also controls where another portion of the bass population may start hanging out.

Not all bass in a lake are the same, just like the different personalities in people. In a population of bass, several different styles of living can be found. Some bass are by nature more aggressive than others. Some prefer life in a school, while others prefer to be by themselves. One school of bass may travel the same half mile route each day to and from feeding areas, while another school will not leave a small pocket in the weeds for days on end.

By and large, bass fishing after spawning is definately related to the first growth of weeds that develops on a lake. I reflect on a trip to northern Michigan where the bass fishing was simply fantastic on some very small lakes. The time was mid June and the reed banks that lined the shores of the lake were just starting to grow above the surface. Anywhere the short spike reeds could be found, I took bass after bass. I figure that over one hundred bass came to the boat during my first day of fishing. This pattern was repeated again and again over the years in Wisconsin and Minnesota as well.

Summertime Bass Habits

As the water warms, the weeds begin to grow and bass fishing is in full swing. Many tournaments are taking place at this time of year, and interest in fishing is high in general. By far one of the most critical ideas to remember about bass fishing really applies to the start of the summer season, but can also help your success at any time of year. It is a rather simple phrase and one which skilled anglers keep in the backs of their minds at all times:

"BASS LOVE THINGS!"

This simple phrase can be your biggest reason for increased bass fishing success. With such a wide variety of "things" found on and in our North Country lakes, I would have a hard time listing all the things to look for.

Tournament fishing is one way to increase your need to find bass. When there are big bucks on the line, tournament anglers will stop at nothing to find a bass. One such occasion in northern Wisconsin opened my eyes to the adaptability of bass in the North Country. One of the things this writer prides himself on is the ability to catch bass from any lake in Yankee country. With a tournament scheduled for mid-summer, I would have time to pre-fish the waters to discover any secret hot spots the lake may offer. As it turned out, all of my conventional methods of fishing resulted in nothing but muskies. In many muskie lakes, the muskies control many of common "bass" spots on this lake. I was frustrated and figured that if I just kept fishing the areas I thought looked good, a bass would come along.

After two days of hard fishing and catching only a few small bass, this fisherman was stumped. As I worked along a shoreline I came across a man and his son fishing from a small boat. Asking the usual question of "catching any?" he responded with a smile, said "no", and asked if the bass were biting. Smiling, I didn't want to lie because my name was in bold letters on the side of the boat, I told him I was having trouble finding bass on this lake. This stranger said he had been fishing the lake for years and had taken all of his bass on the west end of the lake under the bogs. I knew the bogs were there, but for some reason I never spend much time fishing that kind of water. I wasted no time in checking out his tip and he was right. The bogs seemed to hold all the bass in the lake. Since that time I have consistently taken bass from bogs during the late spring, summer, and even in the fall.

Other unique areas you may find on your individual lake could range from old car tires and fence lines to fancy wooden boat houses. Bass love to hang around all sorts of things, and if nothing unique exists in your lake, the bottom contour of the lake is what they will relate to. Fifty years ago my grand father would take my dad to a nearby lake and cast plugs around the fallen trees that lined the shores. This same lake is now almost in downtown Minneapolis and all the trees have been removed. A beautiful grassy lawn now lines the shores. With the increase in lake shore ownership, many fallen trees have been removed to enhance property values.

Bass for years have loved to sit in the limbs of a fallen tree, but with the trees gone, where do the bass find home? The answer is boat docks! The bass moved into the boat docks and found all the comforts of home in these man-made structures. The techniques for actually fishing many of the more common bass hide-outs will be talked about later in a special chapter on tactics.

As summer wears on, bass begin to group in larger and larger schools. This grouping often starts on what is referred to as the inside bends of a drop-off or weed bed. The term inside bend could also be referred to as an inside

17

Night action for bass peaks during the warmest months of the summer. Many anglers who venture out after sundown can take lunkers like this on topwater baits.

Broadleaf **Tobacco Cabbage** **Curly Cabbage**

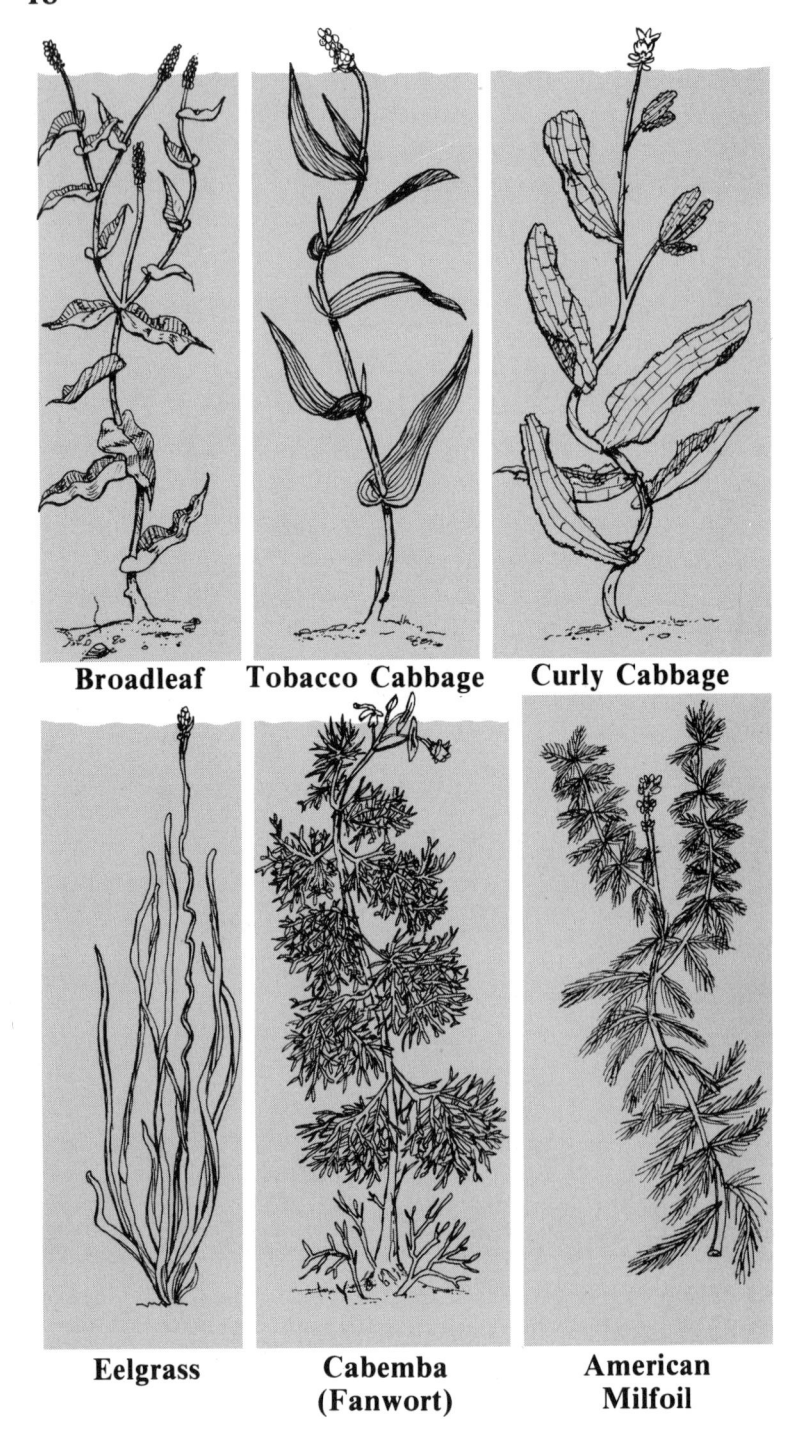

Eelgrass **Cabemba (Fanwort)** **American Milfoil**

Sake Rush **Soft/Hard Stem Bullrush** **White Water Lilly**

Crowsfoot or Buttercup **Waterweed or Ditchmoss** **Stonewort or Sandgrass** **Mare's Tail**

point. This is an area of deeper or clean bottom area extending into an area bordered by shallower or weedy waters, kind of like the reverse of a regular point which may extend out from shore.

Once the bass start to school, they do so by size. This is done mostly to keep competition between bass on a fair level. A one pound bass will want to feed on smaller forms of food than would a five pounder. To appeal to their individual needs they will tend to hang out in different areas.

When schools of bass along a weed edge move about to feed, the direction of their movements are not up and down. They prefer a movement parallel to the edges or drop-offs. For years anglers believed that bass moved up into the shallows to feed and then slipped back into the depths to hold. A hole in this theory was discovered with tracking studies showing that the bass preferred to move laterally almost 80% of the time. Bass would move in and out at the same depth level but move up and down very little when they wanted to feed. This tracking study also showed the individual habits of some bass who preferred to move great distances while others stayed in one area all the time.

As summer slips into what many call the "Dog Days", bass fishing in shallow water can become very difficult unless great amounts of cover for holding bass can be found. Bass can be triggered to strike even on the hottest of August days. Anglers will find that moving to deeper water and using lures that cover water quickly will be the most consistent way to discover the more aggressive schools of bass. In many cases I have seen slower methods of fishing produce nothing, while fast moving baits scored time and time again.

In my own studies on bass schooling behavior, I have found bass in extremely large schools during hot spells. They tend to move around a great deal in what appears to be a quest for easy prey. These schools of late summer bass are the makings of a "honey hole" for sure. The outside weedline edge is where much of the action takes place. Schools of small sunfish often feed heavily just below the surface, and occasionally a northern pike or bass will attack sending them jumping right out of the water. When large schools of sunfish can be seen on the surface, schools of bass are VERY close by. At this time of year, the outside points tend to see more bass activity.

Fall Bass Movements

The summer season will hold well into early September in many cases. The later we get into fall, the more the bass start to fatten up for the long, cold winter ahead. It seems to be a combination of cooler nights and shorter days that gets the bass into this feeding mood. This is by far the time of year when most of the truly big bass are taken.

Often Labor Day in the North Country sees outstanding catches of bass in normal summertime spots. The bass want to feed heavily on all the small panfish and minnows that can be found around the lake. The real fall bass fishing begins as the weeds turn brown and start to die off. To the bass, this means a change in location. Every predator fish in the lake shifts its location because the bait fish move. The dying weeds will force the food fish to other areas. Many baitfish relocate in sandy or rocky areas, while others simply prefer to stay along a windswept shore. Wave action washes food to shore, often in areas with a northern exposure. The cold autumn wind from the north can really stir up a shoreline.

A portion of the bass population will also take advantage of the fall frog migration. In areas with soft, mucky shorelines, the biggest bass you will ever see are cruising in only a foot of water, waiting for a frog to jump in. The key to success here is simply fishing close enough to the bank. I have caught bass with as many as five frogs in their stomachs at one time. To a bass, a live frog is like a prime steak to us fishermen.

This fall period is rather short in many respects and may only last for one month. Like with the spring activity, the bass seem to go crazy, but not too many sportsmen are still on the water at this time.

Fall bass are often fat and sassy. This five pounder was taken from a windswept point, which is a common feeding area for fall bass. Take a special note that this fish was netted and not landed by hand. With big fish, bass anglers use a rubber net to quickly bring the bass into the boat. This is especially true when crankbaits are used. The two sets of treble hooks can be very dangerous if the angler tries to land the bass by hand.

Late Fall Bassin'

The late fall period is so different from the regular fall patterns that I had to separate it from the fall category. The key factor here is when the turnover takes place. Turnover occurs when the water temperature on the surface is cooler than the water at the bottom of the lake. Since warmer water rises, the water from the lake bottom changes place with the colder water on the surface.

This turnover period mixes up the water and makes fish-

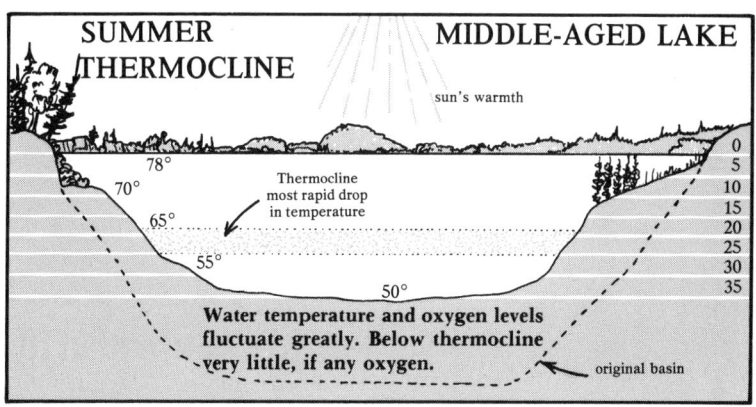

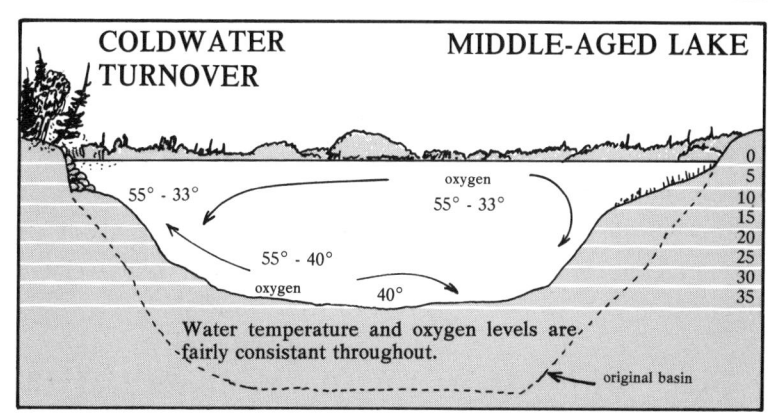

SUMMER THERMOCLINE   **MIDDLE-AGED LAKE**

sun's warmth

78°
70°
65°
Thermocline most rapid drop in temperature
55°
50°

0
5
10
15
20
25
30
35

Water temperature and oxygen levels fluctuate greatly. Below thermocline very little, if any oxygen.

original basin

COLDWATER TURNOVER   **MIDDLE-AGED LAKE**

55° - 33°
oxygen
55° - 33°
55° - 40°
oxygen
40°

0
5
10
15
20
25
30
35

Water temperature and oxygen levels are fairly consistant throughout.

original basin

During the summer, the temperature layer in the water called a thermocline keeps the bass near the weed edge above the cold water. The turnover mixes the water and confuses the bass as to where they should feed. Anglers often avoid these times until the churned-up lake settles down and the bass start feeding on a more regular basis.

ing very difficult. The water mix-up causes the bait fish to scatter. This makes it hard for schools of bass to find food. The big secret here for fishermen is to fish larger lakes late into the fall. These larger lakes are the last to turn over because the larger volume of water takes longer to cool. When the larger lakes start to turn, the smaller lakes are often just completing the turnover stage.

Heavily stained water tells you that turnover is taking place. Often on calm days, you can actually see the water moving, bringing weeds and muck towards the surface. Once the turnover has settled down, the lake becomes very clear.

Fall fishing, after the weeds die off and the water has gone through the turnover stage, is feast or famine. The bass school very tightly together as the water temperature drops. The activity of the bass slows, although they will still feed. Anglers will find fishing the best at mid-day under a clear sky. Similar to fishing very early in the spring, the bass will want to grab smaller lures or lures fished very slowly.

The schools of bass hang around the areas where they will be spending much of the winter. These areas are often in fairly deep water close to shore. A steep drop is one of my personal favorites, especially where there is a sandy shoreline. Often on heavily weeded lakes a few stalks of green weeds will still live. If you can find these areas of deeper green weeds, the bass will never leave them to feed because green weeds will still attract baitfish.

SEASONAL MOVEMENTS OF SMALLMOUTH IN LAKES AND RIVERS

Lake Erie, Lake Michigan, Lake of the Woods, Rainy Lake, and a host of other large lakes offer some of the finest smallmouth bass fishing in the world. Finding and catching bass in these large lakes is not really as difficult as it may sound, however, you must have an understanding of why smallmouth bass move.

When we talk about river smallmouth, we are talking about bass with a completely different outlook on where they live and how they move. River fish simply adjust differently to their moving water environment. Although smallmouth are by nature a river fish, they have adapted to lakes very well in some cases. To make things a little easier to follow, let's start first with lake smallmouth and then discuss the seasonal movements in rivers.

Winter Movements for Smallmouth Bass

This time of year is also a very inactive time for the smallmouth. Just as with the largemouth, the smallmouth are greatly affected by water temperatures. In cold water, the smallmouth are usually found near the deepest part of the lake on the hard, firm bottom. In winter, a smallmouth can spend much of its time in water thirty feet or more in depth. They feed very seldom and do not move more than a few yards all winter.

Wintering smallmouth are often tightly schooled, and like winter largemouth fishing, actually catching them is very difficult. I have seen some fishermen actually snag smallmouth while ice fishing. At first I thought they were lucky, but these avid jig fishermen proceeded to snag six more smallmouth from the same hole, while other lines only a few feet away never saw a fish. Although the fish were caught by accident and all were released, it is a great example of how tightly they school in winter and how little they move even when spooked.

Ice-Out Smallmouth

The key to finding smallmouth bass at ice-out time rests on your ability to fish deep water. The hard bottom areas, close to shore with ready access to deep water, will act as a holding area before the fish move up to spawn. In contrast

Schools of smallmouth are found in the early spring and again in late fall. Anglers who are lucky enough to find these groups of bass experience some fantastic action. Smallmouth, like all schooling fish, prefer to school by size to make the competition for food fair for all members of the group.

to the largemouth, which moves shallow to feed, the smallmouth prefers to stay much deeper. In lakes where both smallmouth and largemouth exist, I have taken largemouth in three feet of water and four pound smallmouth from fifteen feet of water off a rocky shoreline on the same day.

Smallmouth in early spring like to live around objects along the bottom. Many prime smallmouth lakes are very clear. This means the smallmouth will hide in any type of bottom obstruction they can find. It may be a fallen limb or a single big boulder, but as many as a dozen fish may be using it.

Past experience has taught me to start fishing depths where you just lose sight of the bottom. Smallmouth tend to start hitting two to three weeks after the largemouth action starts. This, of course, is in direct relation to the warming of the waters. Generally, smallmouth rarely stray far from the main body of the lake.

Spawning Smallmouth

The smallmouth spawns in deeper water and later than the largemouth, but they both spawn when the water temperatures are in the mid-sixties. The male smallmouth again has the job of building a nest, doing so in a more sloppy manner than the largemouth. A smallmouth likes to hollow out an area around a root or branch. Even a old tire can serve as a good nesting area.

There is a major difference in the spawning behavior of the two bass. A largemouth will leave the nest for good if unfavorable conditions occur. Smallmouth, on the other hand, have been found working spawning beds well into the summer if earlier attempts were spoiled by bad weather.

In many cases, anglers will be fishing blind for the spawners because the nests are often in four to six feet of water. Boat docks are prime areas to hit for large females as they wait to come to the nests. Schools of female smallmouth feel very much at home under docks. They can also be in slightly warmer waters to ripen their eggs. In lakes where you see few boat docks, the females tend to lie just off from the nesting areas.

Spring is one time during the year when smallmouth are shallow enough to take with shallow water bassin' methods such as topwater lures. I have seen bass come up from eight feet of water to grab a topwater lure in a very clear lake. Fishing in such clear water means long casts and light lines to reduce the chance of spooking the bass.

Early Summer Smallmouth

As with all fish, the need for food, security and comfort is very important to the smallmouth. Early summer begins after the bass have come off their nests. This is one of the best times for the bass and the angler. The crayfish is the first love of the smallmouth and early June is when the crayfish start spawning in the North Country. They leave the protection of the rocks to mate and are easy prey for the smallmouth. The bright red colors on a crayfish signal this

An isolated rock island found in the middle of a lake is one of the easiest places to find a school of smallmouth. These small islands often have a ridge extending out from at least one side. This forms a food shelf for the smallmouth to feed and live around. Many a limit of smallmouth has been taken from these isolated islands.

time of year and the smallmouth will gorge themselves.

A secret to finding smallmouth is simply to find the crayfish. They prefer to mate along gravel to sand shores instead of the big boulders where they may live later on in the season, hiding from the smallmouth. These areas of gravel when blown by the wind make for some easy pickings for the smallmouth. The peak times for crayfish activities are at night. Smallmouth prefer to feed on them during the early mornings and evening hours when they start to move. Action during the day could be very poor in the same areas where a bass was taken on every cast at dawn.

Summer Smallmouth Habits

In many of our natural lakes, the habits of summer smallmouth can vary a great deal. On one lake the bass may not move any deeper than ten feet all summer while on others they seldom move shallower than ten feet all year. Basically, lake smallmouth are lovers of big boulders wherever they can find them. If boulders are not present, they take advantage of either deep water or other forms of bottom obstructions to school around. A smallmouth needs to feel secure, but unlike the largemouth who often lives in a world of heavy weeds, the smallmouth prefers open water areas.

A smallmouth school is often smaller in number than summertime largemouth schools. Smallmouth are very tough little guys and don't seem to get along with other fish very well at all. In my pond studies, the smallmouth never grouped in schools of more than two fish and even that was rare. Largemouth in the same pond would be schooling in groups of fifteen to twenty at all times.

Anglers, looking to find smallmouth need only to find some type of deep water objects to fish around. These objects will vary from lake to lake, so the fisherman must keep an open mind.

Fall Smallmouth Movements

The cooling water temperature causes the smallmouth in lakes to go on a feeding binge. In many cases this can be the time for some great bassin'. Lake Erie is quickly gaining a reputation for its outstanding fall fishing for smallmouth. Hugh schools of smallmouth feed on soft shell crays(crayfish), minnows and anything else that gets in their way. This same grouping of smallmouth in other areas also occurs each fall. A bass which is very much a loner, seems to loose their independence as the water temperatures drop and form large schools. This schooling nature means that anglers who fish at this time either catch a limit or nothing at all.

These schools of smallmouth are often found in the deepest areas of hard rock bottom the lake may have. It may be as deep as forty feet deep and the bass could number in the thousands.

Colder water temperatures after the turnover period tend to shut smallmouth action off for the season. The largemouth can still be caught because they stay near shallow water and a single warm day can get them excited enough to strike. The deeper water habits of smallmouth often means that the season for most is over by early November. Although I have personally taken smallmouth in December on a few larger lakes which still have open water, the number of fish taken was small.

River Smallmouth Locations

Much of the original range of the smallmouth bass consisted of river systems. Smallmouth seem to love the rocky clear streams here in the North Country. In rivers, we have several different types of streams that smallmouth can live in. There are the small young rivers which are often very rocky and fast. The middle aged rivers have lots of sand and occasional rock piles. The old rivers, like the lower portions of the Mississippi, which have dredged barge channels with slower moving water.

River smallmouth respond to current the same way in all types of rivers. A river bass never strays far from the current, because to the river bass, the current is what brings them all their food. In any section of river you look at, there are places that are better than others for holding bass. River smallmouth live in a very small world and this attitude of staying in one area can make for some great fishing too. Unfortunately, river fishing in general is not all that popular with the everyday bass angler. In many ways river bass fishing is far more consistent and easier to learn than lake fishing for smallmouth.

Winter Smallmouth in Rivers

River smallmouth winter in the deepest holes that they can find. Smallmouth hate any kind of current, so they often lay tight along the bottom in these deep holes and don't move all winter. Close to 80% of all the smallmouth in a short stretch of river will be sitting in the same hole all winter long and anglers fishing these areas will never get a bite.

Ice-Out Smallmouth

The spring thaw is not a pleasant thought for the river smallmouth. For rivers, the moving water will be the first to open up, but this movement of water means it will stay cooler long after the ice has come off the lakes, because the icy run-off of snow keeps them high, dirty and cold well into May.

Unless you are able to find an area on the river which is isolated from fresh run-off and dirty water, the chances of finding smallmouth action is almost nil. Until water levels stabilize, the chances of finding any concentrations of smallmouth are very slim. The water must reach the mid fifties in the main channel before you can expect to see much smallmouth activity.

River Smallmouth in the Spring

Since the rivers often warm much slower than many lakes, the smallmouth is often up to two weeks behind their lake counterparts. Life is tough on the river smallmouth at this time of year with changing water levels almost every day. If the water levels can stabilize, the smallmouth will move to the back side of a pool or eddy current very close to shore. In some areas there may also be small cuts or channels off the main channel that the smallmouth may slip into.

One very interesting thing about smallmouth at any time of year is their ability to detect changes in water levels. This is especially true in the spring, when they may move to the back side of a quiet channel for a day or so, but if the water levels drop only a few inches, they head back to the main channel.

Strangely enough, the larger females seem to be the most aggressive at this time of year and many anglers see some real dandy smallmouth. The bass will never be found in areas surrounded by current, rather in areas where they can lay next to either a dead water area or shore.

Spawning River Smallmouth

Unlike their lake counterparts who often have access to deep water almost at will, the river fish are not so lucky. In many of the younger rivers where the maximum depth might be only ten feet, deep is a relative term. Spawning smallmouth seem to know that the river levels change. Maybe that is why they are capable of spawning more than one time a year if conditions are not right. A "normal" spring doesn't seem to come along very often these days and if river smallmouth were not able to adapt, they would not be around for long.

Quiet backwater areas with gravel bottoms seemed to be

preferred by the smallmouth. They very seldom build their own nests more than fifty yards from some type of current.

Since deeper water often doesn't exist, the smallmouth can be found spawning in only a foot of water. The spawning time is the one time where you might only catch one fish from a fantastic looking pool. This is because they are very territorial. Like the largemouth in lakes, the smallmouth like to be by themselves for the spawning period and anglers may need to cover a lot of water to catch a limit of bass.

Summer Smallmouth in Rivers

Once the spawning as been completed, the smallmouth in rivers really never school tightly together. They prefer to take up positions along eddie currents and feed more as individuals than in schools. Each bass positions their bodies behind a rock or other obstruction in the current and waits for something good to swim or crawl by. In the river bottoms of the Mississippi, the smallmouth often sit in the shoreline areas that have been lined with rocks about the size of a basketball. These areas are of course man made and are called rip-rap. Personally, one of my favorite areas would be the uprooted trees just off the main channels. Here, in the protection of the roots, some of the largest smallmouth live.

The mating season for the crayfish also takes place in rivers and the smallmouth take full advantage of it too. In a river though, a smallmouth really never travels very far for the whole summer. Any obstruction of current will play a vital part in the life of a smallmouth.

Having grown up on the Upper Mississippi River, one of the first tricks I ever learned about river smallmouth was to use the current and my own body to become a place to catch bass. Just by standing in the same spot while I fished, the smallmouth would soon start using my own legs to hide behind!

Dandy smallmouth like this came from behind some bridge supports. These places on any river can be prime holding areas for smallmouth. These were taken from below a major highway that thousands of people use every day. Many of the best river smallmouth spots are the most obvious.

Fall Smallmouth in Rivers

Fall is by far the best time of year to be fishing smallmouth on rivers. The water levels are often the lowest of the year, and the smallmouth are packed into tighter groups because of the lower water levels.

Fishing moving water is a challenge at anytime, and the more water you have flowing, the tougher it gets. This is why many of the avid river rats do most of their fishing when other anglers are complaining about the "dog days of summer". River fishing has peaked and any type of current break is capable of holding a bass at one time or another. Past experience has shown me that the deepest stretches of river will hold the largest bass. Many anglers can catch a hundred smallmouth per day from the shallow faster waters. The bigger fish tend to prefer the deeper and slower portions of the river, but access to current is STILL a major priority.

Late Fall and River Smallmouth

When we talk of late fall, we are generally referring to the last weeks in October and the first half of November. These days are often very good for the guys who are still willing to wet a line. Rivers never experience the turnover like lakes, so many anglers who can't fish their favorite

Fall smallmouth often group behind dams on rivers which offer few deep water holding areas. With the use of live bait, many of the largest smallmouth can be tricked into striking well into November.

lake take to the rivers for a few weeks and have some great fun.

Water temperature is once more a critical factor in your ability to find aggressive bass. Many of the the smaller pools where you had taken bass during the summer are only holding walleyes now. Only some of the largest and deepest pools in a river will hold bass. Nature has taught them to seek out areas that will not freeze solid over the winter or force them to fight any current.

The time frame for actually catching these smallmouth while they are still willing to grab a lure may last only a week or two, but fishing can be simply fantastic.

CHAPTER THREE

SHALLOW WATER BASSIN' TACTICS

One of the pure joys of bass fishing is to see a largemouth or smallmouth leap from the water with your lure securely in it's jaw. Catching both types of bass in shallow water is a thrill that warms the hearts and memories of avid anglers come January.

Shallow water fishing has gone through many cycles of popularity in recent years, with all the press given to "structure fishing". Deep water bass in many lakes were left untapped as anglers become hooked on one way of fishing and forgot all others. Suddenly they would rediscover that bass like lily pads, and the cycle would start over again.

Tournament fishermen often set the pace for many anglers across the country. When deep water bassin' first became popular, many of the shoreline fishermen started fishing the drop-offs. This new craze of the "scientific" methods of fishing changed the strategies of many good fishermen. Unfortunately, the jury is still out looking to find all of the answers in how to catch bass.

I remember a seminar a few years back when one of the big bass boys from down south came north to let us in on what was really going on in the big tournaments. This well-known bass angler was quick to point out that all of the gobbledy-goop that we read about is just hype to make people think that they really know what they're doing. The fact of the matter is, that with all of the knowledge about deep water bassin', and all of that "scientific" junk, everybody still beats the shorelines ninety percent of the time anyway!

History has shown that the majority of our current bass fishing methods came from the southern regions of the

United States. Many of the razzle-dazzle lures with lots of bells and whistles win a few tournaments down south and, before you know it, the North Country anglers begin to use them as well.

Fads in bass fishing methods may come and go, but shallow water bass fishing will always be a great way to go. Let's first decide what "shallow water" is. In theory, you

The largemouth bass is truly the sportfish of the 80's, and more and more anglers in the North Country are finding this out.

could be in ten feet of water that is choked with weeds and still use shallow water tactics because you may only have one foot of open water above the weeds in which to present your lure. Shallow water, to me, is water that is one to four feet deep. The lures you select to fish with will often work for both smallmouth and largemouth bass. The difference in water types will often indicate which species we are most likely to find.

Bottom content is the key to your success in shallow water bassin'. Some areas of sand may hold fish at dawn, but you can bet that the bass will not hold in this area come mid-day. This brings us to the importance of selecting areas which have unique bottom shapes or contents.

Smallmouth bass, for example, love to feed in areas of softball to basketball sized rock with some wind pounding the area. But when they hold for the rest of the day, they seek out larger boulders the size of bushel baskets.

Largemouth are weed lovers by nature, but will move to areas free from weeds when the light conditions are low and especially when a brisk wind is blowing into an area. The rest of the time you can bet they are cruising areas with thicker weed growth. The thicker the weeds, the better the chances of the fish holding there all day long.

There are, of course, countless combinations of shallow water bottom structure and content that can hold bass, and it would be impossible for me to list every possible situation that you may encounter. Let me just say that learning to read "visual structure" is the key to your success in shallow water fishing. Both types of bass love to hang around things which are unique and different. By visually spotting these areas, you can consistently catch bass from shallow water areas.

Lure selection can actually be made from four different types of lures. Knowing which will be the most effective is really based on your success each day. You must learn to select the proper lure to match the situation and many times this can only be done by a little trial and error. Once you have selected one particular lure or method, keep an open mind to others that may be equally effective. Once you cover an area with one presentation, you may want to go back over the same water with a different lure or method that could appeal to bass that are in a different mood.

The attitude of a feeding bass can change several times during a day. In the morning they maybe riding high, as the sun rises, they could move deeper into the same weedbed. That is way anglers must be willing to try a variety of different lure types to best reach the bass.

TOP WATER: This category of lures has a lot of colorful history behind it. Many of the first plugs that were invented were top water lures used to catch bass. Whenever I think of top water baits, I think of a story I heard a long time ago about Buck Perry, who is considered to be the "father of structure fishing." Buck was traveling around the country promoting his new lures and methods of fishing when he came face to face with another promoter who was jumping up and down about the effectiveness of his company's new top water lure. His bold statements and photos made a very convincing argument, but Mr. Perry boldly stated that he could catch more and bigger fish with a plain old stick. Buck knew from past experiences that the way a lure is presented is often more important than the name on the label. Taking a stick found along the shore and attaching some hooks, he set out to catch a pile of bass. Needless to say he scored big and the lure promoter left town eating his words.

This little story is a living example of why many lures do most of their catching before they even get wet! You can be a very effective bass fisherman in shallow or deep water just by learning to fish a handful of different lures.

Choosing a Top Water Lure

Top water lures with spinners on the front, back or both ends seem to be slightly more effective than ones without when there is a slight chop on the water. Many top water baits having a blunt nose which can be chugged or twitched, are best when the water is like glass.

Another factor that can play an important part in your success is selecting a top water lure of the appropriate size. The rule is simple: the more stained the water, the larger the lure you should use. Many of our gin-clear North Country lakes make it very difficult to fish top water lures successfully. Your only chance is to be fishing at dawn or at dusk when the light levels are low and the bass cannot see as well. Another option is to fish areas on the lake that have very heavy weed cover. Larger bass feel more secure when they are hiding under or in some weeds. This knowledge will make it possible for you to get your baits close to the bass without frightening them.

Selecting the proper lure color can be a real can of worms. The more spooked the fish are, the more important it is to use a light colored top water lure. When a bass looks upwards, the sky is very light colored. A large, dark object flying towards a five pound bass will send it darting away. It is very difficult to cast your lure near a super shallow bass. When this situation presents itself, it is often best to select a light colored lure. Dawn and dusk fishing is a low light time. The bass are in a more aggressive mood and are less likely to be spooked. A lure that stands out from the background of the sky can be effective at this time. A top water lure with a combination of black and yellow is one of my personal favorites.

For me, lure shape has never been much of a problem. The short, chunky top water lures tend to make more of a splash as opposed to those shaped like a cigar. Lure size can be another factor to your success in catching spooked fish. As a rule, the smallest, lightest top water baits are best for those super clear water situations, but casting accuracy with light lures can be very challenging. By staying with the heavier, cigar-shaped top water lures anglers should be able to reach bass successfully in most situations.

The techniques for fishing top water bass involve many different factors. Line size should not exceed eight pound test in areas of open water. This is especially true in smallmouth fishing when you are fishing above the rocky bottom and the bass can see more of the surface when they come up to attack. Largemouth, on the other hand, often are found in areas of dense cover. In this situation you will want to use at least fourteen pound test. The heavier line is used more out of necessity, because once you hook a big bass in thick cover, you will need all the line strength possible to pull her out.

43

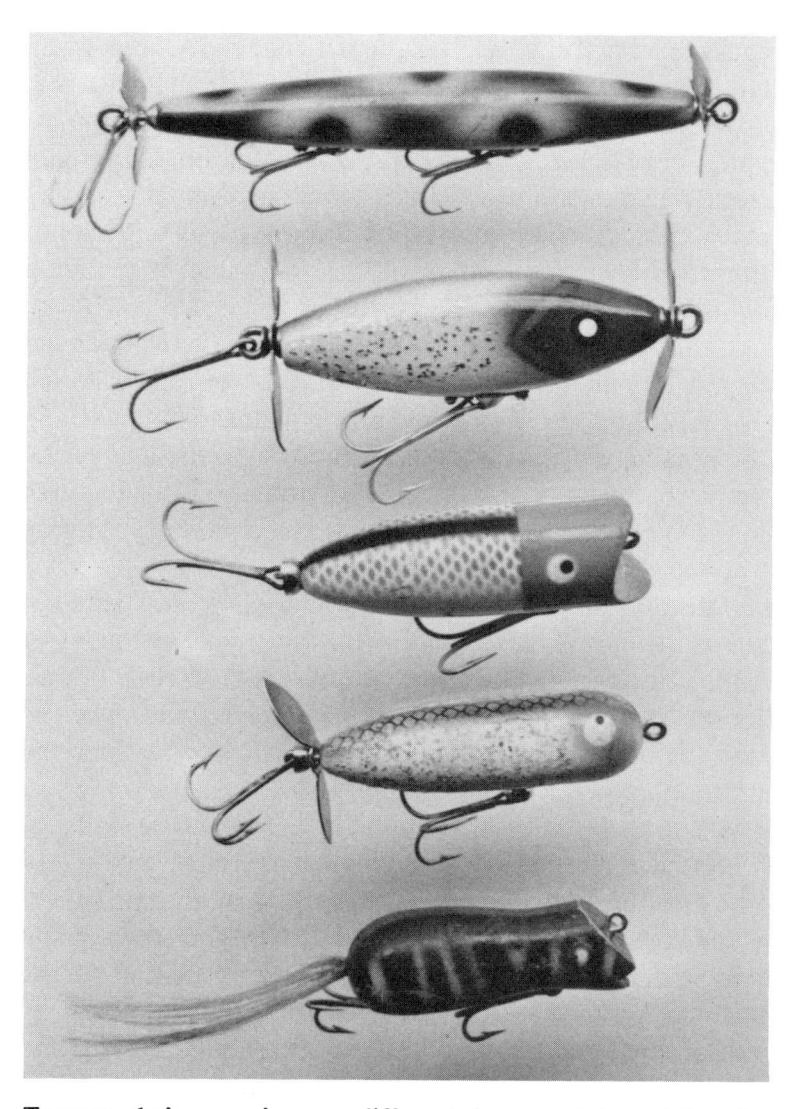

Topwater baits come in many different shapes and sizes. All can be productive, and each will give you a different topwater action. From top to bottom we have the Devils Horse (Smithwick), Little Lucky Dog (Shakespeare), Lucky 13 (Heddon), Baby Torpedo (Heddon), and the Meadow Mouse (Creek Chub).

The longer your casts, the better, because you are looking for bass that are riding high above the weeds or in the rocks. You will easily spook them if your casts are not well out in front of the boat. Unfortunately, you can have a real problem in making long casts with accuracy. Often you will see a pocket in the weeds, a log, or a boulder which could be holding a bass. Unless your cast is on target, you can bet that the fish will not be willing to travel much more than one foot from either side of the object it is hiding behind.

Exactly how a top water lure is fished varies from day to day. Many anglers who fish top water lures regularly will use the "do nothin'" method of top water fishing early in the season. The colder water slows down the aggressive strikes of the bass, and the only way that you can get them to grab your lure is to simply let it float on the surface for up to one minute each time it is moved!

This may sound like a boring way to fish, but it is full of suspense. The biggest bass you may ever take on top water lures could come at this time. With a light twitch, followed by the "do nothin'" period, you get the attention of the bass. It seems that the longer you wait, the madder she gets!

The ever popular "Jitterbug" is one top water bait that will be in tackle boxes long after all of us are gone. This unique lure sputters and gurgles its way along the surface. A steady retrieve is most often used with the Jitterbug, and it can be deadly! A Jitterbug type of lure is one that can be extremely effective in areas which are almost too thick and full of cover to cast to a particular target. A steady and noisy retrieve could trigger a strike from a bass anywhere along the course of your retrieve.

Another lure that comes close to the category of the sputtering top water baits is the "popper". Just as the name suggests, the popper is a lure which has a cupped nose and creates a popping sound when given a snap from the rod tip. Popper baits are very effective for the first three feet of their retrieve, and from that point on their effectiveness declines. Poppers are great in areas of deeper brush where that even the biggest of bass will hear it and have plenty of time to come up for a look. For more consistent success use smaller poppers. As with all top water lures, the size of the bait has no effect on the size of the bass you could catch. In many ways, you are best to keep your lures small to better appeal to a finicky bass.

The third group of top water baits is what I like to call the "twitch" baits. These lures are designed to be fished slowly with a twitching motion for the best effect. I refer to the Devils Horse, Bass-O-Reno, Spook, Super Frog and my childhood favorite, the Creek Chub Mouse.

As a youngster, I found that the Creek Chub Mouse was deadly. I had developed a special technique of shaking my rod tip to make the bait just quiver on the surface. This wobbling action drove the bass crazy! As time went by, I began using many of the more up to date baits such as the Super Frog and the Devils Horse.

As I began writing this section, my notes called for describing the use of various top water baits. I ran down to my private pond in my back yard to try that old Creek Chub Mouse that I had used as a kid. It seemed like old times, putting on my mouse, although it did have a little rust on the hooks from sitting in my tackle box for the last fifteen years.

On my first cast a two pound bass leaped right out of the water after it, and all I had done was to let it lie on the water without moving it. The next fish came the same way, and after three more nice fish I began to remember just how effective this bait had been for me as a kid. I know it may sound strange, but I have so much confidence in a Devils Horse, that I decided to take off the mouse and make a few casts with the "Horse." After five minutes and not even a swirl, I put the mouse on again, and almost as if they were waiting there to grab it, I took three fish on as many casts!

Needless to say, it was very difficult to come back in and begin writing again, (I really enjoy conducting all this in-depth research that comes with writing a book). Having written two very successful books already, I have experienced this with each of them as I try to describe in words how I fish. In helping others to fish, I have become keenly aware of the little things that many people overlook.

Twitch baits, as I like to call them, are really not designed to be fished in any other way than slow. In most cases you are also "spot" fishing. You need to pick out an area or opening in the weeds and drop your lure into a tea cup. The lure is left there until the ripples subside. Then twitch your rod tip to make the lure wobble to life. Repeat this process two or three times and then simply reel the lure quickly to the boat and look for another target.

The Bass Oreno and the Creek Chub Mouse are two very popular examples of top water baits that can also be used effectively just under the surface as a swimming bait. This makes for a multi-purpose lure which can be fished as a "twitch" bait first, and later in the same retrieve as a shallow running lure.

Another version of the twitch lures is the Heddon Spook type of lure which has a rounded nose to permit a "walking the dog" action as it is twitched along the surface. This unique side-to-side action can draw strikes all through the retrieve. This is very effective when used over a lot of thick cover because it can really draw a bass up from deep water. This action can be easily made if you drop your rod tip towards the water, and as you reel in slowly, pump your rod tip with short jerks. Each bait tends to run a little differently, so you will have to get the feel of each as you begin fishing.

The basic rule in top water fishing is to have patience in everything you do. Don't be in a hurry to do anything! This is true in the way you fish a bait and the way you set the hooks as well. Many anglers think that there isn't much to know about hooking a bass when you can see them strike, but getting the hooks into a bass not that simple.

When a bass breaks the surface to grab your bait, you have to make sure of two things before you try to set the hooks. First you need to know if the bass has the bait. The big splash you may see is not the bass swimming away with the bait, but the bass coming up to grab it. If you set the hooks when you see a splash, you will miss eighty percent of your strikes! In shallow water, the bass may not make a splash at all. You may actually see the back of the bass roll on the surface around the bait.

All of these strikes are very exciting, and they happen within a split second, similar to a pheasant flushing from below your feet when you least expect it. The secret is to be aware of what is happening but to try to not set the hooks! It is very easy for me to say this in print, but in real life it is one of the most challenging things to master. Only after you have a few misses under you belt will you begin to realize that you must wait if you want to hook that striking bass.

Pausing for a second or two after you see a splash is extremely critical, but of equal importance is to have a good angle for a hookset. One tip that I was told as a youngster was to never set the hooks until you feel the bass pull back. This may happen five or six seconds after the splash, but a bass will often not be in too much a hurry to drop the bait because it still thinks of it as dinner. Five or six seconds may seem a little like overdoing it, but setting the hooks too late has never been a major problem for anyone I have known.

The reason for the pause is not to let the bass swallow the bait. The reason we must pause after a strike is to get a better angle for the hookset. A bass can come at a top water bait from a variety of angles, and if you try to set the hooks as the fish is swimming towards you, the strike will be

One of the more effective topwater baits in heavy cover is the Super Frog. Note the wire weed guard that protects the hook. It is critical that this small piece of wire be bent to protect the hook at all times.

missed! That is why the rule of waiting until you feel the bass before you strike is a wise rule. If you set on sight alone you may miss your angle, and the bass will either throw the hooks or leave you without a fish at all.

I often suggest fishing with your rod tip pointed up at eleven o'clock at all times if you tend to set the hooks too early. This will force you to give the fish time to grab and turn with the bait as you must drop the tip before you set the hooks. Even the short time it takes to drop your rod tip and raise it for a hookset can make all the difference in the world!

In customizing your lures, there are certain things that you can do to make them more weedless, but to not affect your hooksetting power. One is to cut off the bottom hook if your lure has treble hooks. The other two hooks will ride up next to the body while you pull it over weeds. This can make some lures twice as fishable.

It is possible to remove one of the hooks from a treble with a pair of wire cutters. In heavy cover, this will make any topwater bait more weedless. The two remaining hooks ride up against the body of the bait as it is moved. This trick will not limit the hooking ability of your lure in any way.

Past experience has shown me that top water lures can be extremely effective even when they have only a single hook on the back of the lure! Many people believe that the more you have of anything in life, the better it is, but this is just not so.

The way a top water lures floats in the water can have a great affect on the way it can be fished. Some lures, such as the Heddon Spook, can be modified with lead weights to make it float with its nose up or down in the water to imitate a dying baitfish. Personal experience has shown me that low-riding top water baits are better hookers and tend to attract more strikes. The deeper a bait floats in the water, the easier it is for the fish to grab it successfully.

Top water fishing can be a very addicting way to catch bass. Fly rod fishing with small poppers is great sport as well. I still daydream about the limits of four pound smallmouth I took on my fly rod one June morning. Life can't get much better than that!

THE ART OF SPINNERBAITING

Several years ago spinnerbait fishing was such an important part of my bass fishing success that I wrote one of my very first feature stories for the Fins and Feathers magazine entitled, "The Art of Spinnerbaiting." I liked the title for the story because it said it all. The skills and tactics used in fishing a lure called the spinnerbait IS a form of art.

To the angler, the spinnerbait is a category of lures which represents names such as Buzz Bullet, Lunker Buzz, Scorpion, Reed Runner, Bass Harasser, Hawaiian Wiggler, and the ever popular Beetle-Spin. This family of lures doesn't have the tackle shop sex appeal that a fancy topwater plug which has a photo finish of a bluegill might have. A spinnerbait is a rather strange contraption that consists of a spinner on a wire shaft that is bent like a safety pin. On the other end of the wire is often a big, bushy skirt hiding a rather substantial hook. Spinnerbaits come in many different sizes and shapes. In or out of the water, they really don't resemble an actual form of food, to my knowledge. Some lures look like a mouse or a frog, a minnow or a crayfish, but not the spinnerbait.

If we were to look up the ingredients of a good lure we would need good vibration, action, flash, visibility, and fishability. With these features a spinnerbait is perfect! So, finally fishermen have a lure built to appeal to the fish instead of the fishermen. The pulsating rubber skirt, the spinning blades, the sparkling colors, and its almost weedless nature makes it one of the most versatile shallow water bass baits you could select.

The difference between many good lures and the great ones is that some lures are just plain easy to fish, while others demand a certain amount of practice and experience. First time bass anglers can catch fish by just casting and retrieving a spinnerbait with little regard for how or why it works. A spinnerbait is by no means a lazy man's lure. To

You can't help but be all smiles when a chunky four pound largemouth grabs your spinnerbait. This kind of action can be experienced by anglers of all experience levels because a spinnerbait is just plain tough to fish wrong.

make any lure productive, it has to be kept in the water.

Currently, there are over one hundred different versions

of the spinnerbait. There are spinnerbaits that are only 1/16 of an ounce, and some that are over three ounces. The majority of spinnerbaits on the market have either one or two spinners. They are referred to as being single or tandem spin spinnerbaits. The action and performance of a single spin over a tandem spin can have a great affect on your success in catching bass. Tandem spinners make it possible for you to fish the lure faster and right on the surface. Single spins, surprisingly enough, give off about as much vibration, but can be used more effectively in deeper water and for slower retrieves. Many of the more advanced spinnerbait throwers prefer the use of a single spin over the tandem because they can make the lure perform better under a wide variety of situations.

The actual design of the spinner can have a great effect on your ability to fish a spinnerbait in some areas. There are basically four designs on the market today and of course companies have come up with countless variations to make their lures more effective than other makes.

PROPELLER BLADES These blades are limited to use directly on the surface of the water. They are designed not to give off vibrations, but to slap and sputter across the surface to attract a strike. They should be fished rather fast, right on the surface, so that they throw water as they move along. Often referred to as "Buzzers," these spinnerbaits are deadly in areas of very thick and shallow weeds. The use of the buzzer baits down south is rather extensive, but here in the North Country, they are not known as being a very consistent fish producer.

WILLOW LEAF BLADES This spinner design has the least amount of "lift" to keep the lure near the surface. This is fine if you are fishing in rivers for smallmouth or over deeper weeds in a clear lake. A willow leaf blade is the least popular of all the spinners used today, but it is the easiest of all blade shapes to pull through the water. These spinners are commonly used on the in-line spinners such as the Mepps.

INDIANA BLADES The Indiana blade offers several times more lift than the Willow Leaf blade to keep your baits near the surface. But is also several times more difficult to pull through the water. Often used on tandem spins, the Indiana blades are commonly found on many of the larger sized spinnerbaits.

COLORADO BLADES Most manufacturers use this blade for spinnerbaits because it gives maximum lift and a high amount of vibrations that bass can detect. Ranging in size like the other spinner shapes, from very tiny to a large #8 size blade. You can vary the performance of any spinnerbait to a great degree just by changing the blade size. The larger Colorado blades push quite a bit of water as they move. A spinnerbait with this blade can make a wake on the surface, but actually be several inches below. This rounded spinner is also the most difficult to drag through the water. This is a disadvantage, but this spinnerbait can also be kept very close to the surface at extremely slow speeds, making for a very tempting morsel to bass.

The basic rule in fishing a spinnerbait is to keep the blades in sight at all times. This is why many anglers like to fish them around visual structures found in shallow water. A spinnerbait casts well and can be brought through some of the thickest weeds and brush without snagging. The use of polarized sunglasses is an absolute must for the avid shallow water angler. You will be better able to control the actions of a spinnerbait if you can watch it come towards you through the entire retrieve.

By keeping your rod tip high, you will be able to keep the blades spinning high in the water. This makes it possible to run a spinnerbait just below the surface at very slow speeds. Time and time again, this has been one of the most effective ways to fish a spinner, high and slow.

The type of outfit you use for throwing spinnerbaits will vary, depending on the water to be fished. In heavy cover,

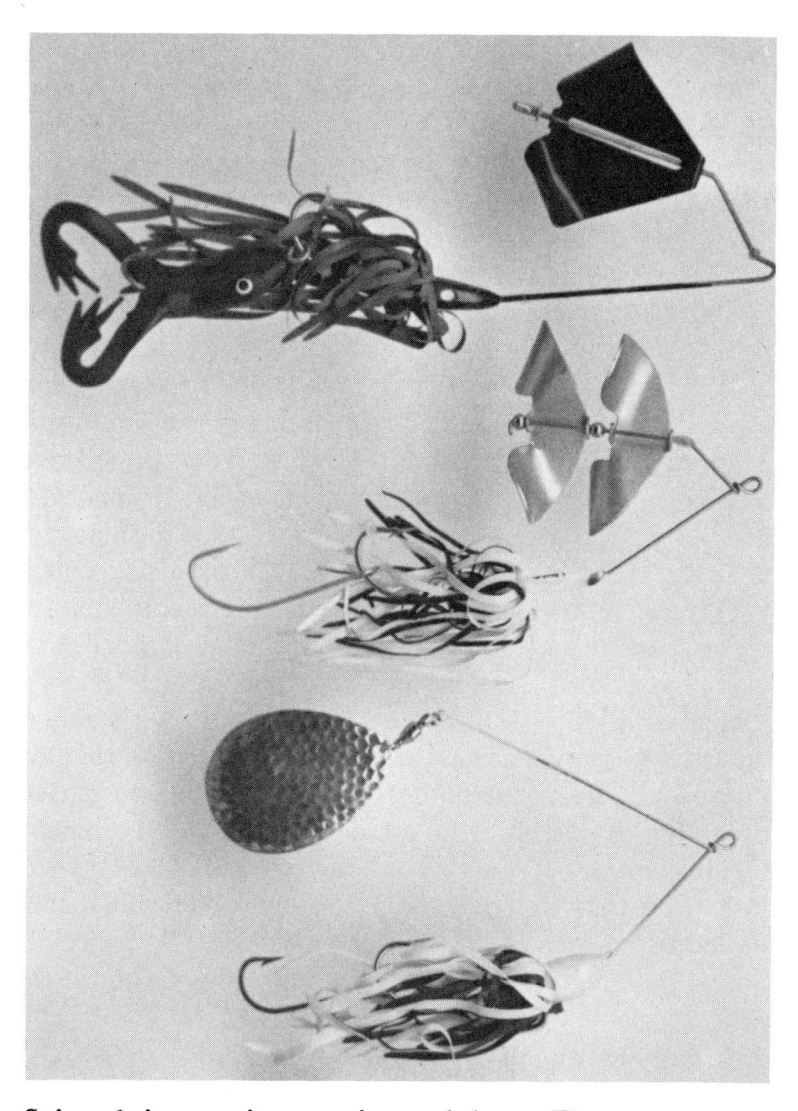

Spinnerbaits come in many sizes and shapes. The two on top are considered to be buzzers with their prop-like blades that churn up the surface. The typical spinnerbait on the bottom can have one or two blades.

it is often best to use a heavier spinnerbait. This is especially true in reed areas because the stalks of reeds will keep a light spinnerbait from reaching the water. From the same vein, the heavier the cover, the heavier the line and tackle you should use.

Many of the buzzer-type baits are tough to throw because the blade spins as it flies through the air and slows it down. I have found open faced spinning tackle to be the best answer to throwing these light spinners. More conventional bait casting gear is a wise idea for most spinners over 1/4 ounce in size. This casting gear can handle heavy lines, and with the high speed gears found in them today, they can be less tiring to use.

With even with the lightest of spinnerbaits, anglers should not use line much lighter than eight pound test. Many avid bass anglers use seventeen or twenty pound test all season long without any problems at all. In fact, the heavier the line you use, the easier it is to keep the baits up near the surface. The larger diameter of the line creates additional water resistance to slow the drop of your lure. In all my years of spinnerbaiting, I have never noticed line visibility as being a problem with spinnerbait fishing. Unlike other lures which may run better with a smaller diameter line, spinnerbaits seem to work better with heavy line! One of the big advantages of heavy line other than its durability, is your ability to get the large hooks of a spinnerbait into the jaw of a bass. The heavier the line, the less the line will stretch, and the more force you will be able to put on the fish during the hookset.

Tuning Your Spinnerbaits

Just about any artificial lure on the market today will need to be "tuned" to some extent in order to work properly. Some companies provide lures that are tank tested to make sure they are running true from the very beginning. Spinnerbaits often run perfectly right from the package, but under normal fishing conditions can become bent out of tune. This is easy to detect because you will notice the bait rolling or running sideways through the water during the retrieve. All spinnerbaits should run with the blade straight above the hooks at all times.

Tuning a spinnerbait is not difficult. There is no need to throw a perfectly good bait away simply because a bass bent it all out of shape. By grabbing the hook and rubber skirt of the bait, bend the wire in the direction the lure is rolling. You may need to check the adjustment with a short cast and re-adjust again. While tuning your lure, take time to check your knot because you will be tying directly to the spinnerbait for best results. Also take special note of the last two feet of line above the lure. Many times the spinnerbait will roll as it is cast and may nick or damage your line.

The large hooks found on most spinnerbaits need to be very strong, but this can prove to be a disadvantage if you don't keep those hooks razor sharp. It may sound as if I'm a bit picky, but in an average year it is common for many

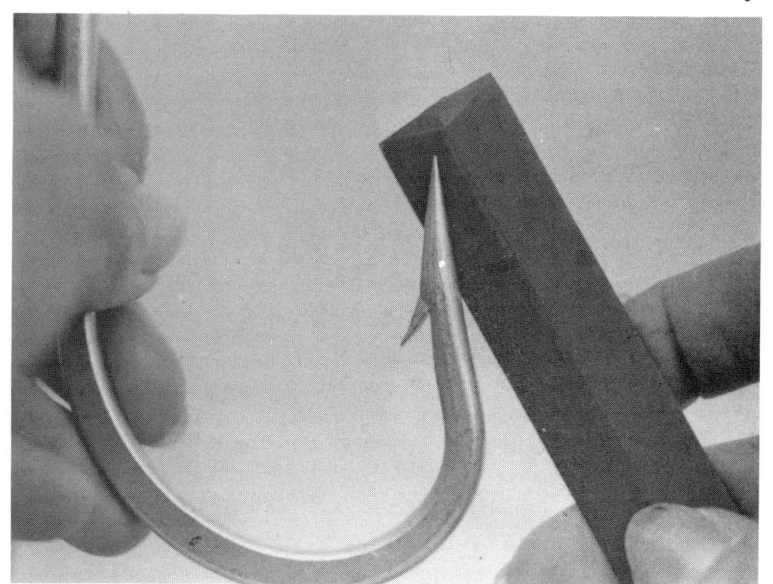

Sharp hooks are one of the easiest ways to start catching more bass. You can use a fine file or stone to sharpen your hooks to a razor sharp finish. Work only the outside of the point and work the sharpening device only towards the eye of the hook. It is a good practice to sharpen every hook in your tackle box, no matter how new a lure is.

anglers to loose up to 30 fish from having weak knots, damaged line, or dull hooks.

Spinnerbaiting Retrieves.

The spinnerbait is best suited to get out there and cover water. Many of our shallow water lakes that are full of weeds can be difficult to fish with any other lure. Sure you could fish a topwater bait slowly and carefully along the bank, but it could take all day just to cover a block of shoreline. The spinnerbait is one of the best shallow water tools for the tournament angler who is looking for a concentration of shallow water fish. Once they are found, a wide variety of methods can be used to concentrate on the school of fish.

What makes the spinnerbait family so effective is that they can be used in a wide variety of situations and with a wide variety of different retrieves. While out fishing you may discover a variation of a technique you will read about in this book, and that is great! It is impossible for me to describe all the methods or styles a spinnerbait is fished.

For a good foundation on spinnerbaiting tactics I feel there are four major ways to fish a spinnerbait effectively. These being the Buzz, Yo-Yo, Stop-Go, and Brush Bombing. In the course of a year each of these methods of fishing a spinnerbait will be effective, and it is a very good idea to have them in the back of your mind at all times.

The Buzz

This retrieve is one that many first time spinnerbait fishermen should start with. The Buzz method of fishing a spinnerbait is by far one of the most popular.

The Buzz is a noisy, attention getting retrieve. Therefore, Buzz baits or tandem spins should be used to give you maximum noise vibrations. The Buzzer baits run very high in the water and seems to appeal to bass which are very aggressive. The tandem spin spinnerbaits run an inch or two deeper in the water and will appeal to more fish. Since they run deeper, the bass will be in a better position to grab your lure successfully.

The term "buzz" does a fine job of describing just how the bait must come through the water. The high speed gears in many of the newer reels are a real blessing. Your goal is to keep your bait moving just below the surface almost as fast as you can turn the reel handle! For these fast retrieves, keep your rod tip at water level while retrieving. The angle of the rod stops the blades of the spinnerbait from breaking the surface, while creating a bulging effect on the water's surface. This bulging effect is what drives the bass crazy.

Another secret to making this technique pay off is to get the bait moving towards you as soon as it hits the water. This is true with all the methods of spinnerbait fishing we will discuss, but doubly important in making "the buzz" effective. You may want to engage your reel even before it hits the water because that spinnerbait should never sink more than a few inches below the surface before it starts coming towards the boat.

Past experience has shown me that using light 1/4 ounce tandem spinnerbaits is a wise choice. Lighter tandems will be easier to keep near the surface and the smaller blades found on these baits will not have as much water resistance. You will be able to fish longer without getting worn out.

One variation of the buzz technique is to simply slow the retrieve down, but keep the blades right near the surface. To do this you again must get the bait moving towards you as soon as it hits the water, but this time keep your rod tip up so the spinners can do more fluttering. You will be able to see 80% of your strikes, and keeping your rod tip high prevents you from setting the hooks too soon. You will need to drop the tip to set the hooks properly, and that is often all the time you will need. This slower version of the buzz is often effective over deeper water when the fish need more time to react to your lure.

Yo-Yo

Good feel and control of your spinnerbait is a must when using this appealing retrieve. The single spin versions of a spinnerbait work best. Only when you are in very shallow water should a light tandem, such as a 1/4 ounce, be

Fishing a spinnerbait above a weedy flat is often a great way to call a big bass up to strike. This six pounder was taken with a modified spinnerbait that had an extra large blade. The blade made it possible for the bait to be fished slower, giving the bass more time to react to the lure and to strike.

used.

Bass found in areas of thick weeds, logs, or boulders are ideal for what I refer to as "pocket bass fishing". Pocket bass tend to stay in these areas all day long, even through cold front conditions. I have found that bass will not move in and out of these areas as they might if they were on the edge of a weedline or drop-off.

Although a bass may be hiding in a pocket of the weeds, the time of day and the current weather conditions can play a big part in their willingness to come up and strike. That is why the yo-yo technique is great for coaxing even the most stubborn fish into striking.

First off, the use of polarized sunglasses plays a major role in your success in using the yo-yo technique. Not only will you want to visually control your spinnerbait, but it is more important than ever that you see the pockets and holes in the bottom vegetation that may be holding the bass.

Your casts should not be made too far from the boat because it will be more difficult to control the actions of your lure. When the spinnerbait hits the water, get it moving towards you as quickly as possible with your rod tip high. At this point, your lure is traveling towards you just below the surface at a very slow pace. You will need to quickly drop your rod tip as your lure passes over an object or pocket in the weeds. Remember that the angle you have on the water can make it hard to judge exactly where the pocket is, so it may take a little practice at first.

By the time you are able to reel up the slack created as you dropped your rod tip, you will be ready to raise the bait back up to the surface once more. You will need to quickly raise the rod tip and increase your reeling pace. If you do it right, the lure can drop and rise again within two feet!

You may want to pause the bait for only a split second over the pocket instead of letting it drop out of sight. On the other hand, if weather conditions such as a cold front push the fish deep into the weeds, you may be forced to let it drop well into the weeds to get a strike.

Stop-Go

As you develop a feel in casting and retrieving, slight variations in retrieves can make a big difference in your ability to trigger a fish into striking. In many ways the "stop-go" method of fishing a spinnerbait is a very short version of the "yo-yo" technique.

You will often find that the little things you discover can be the answers to many angling problems. One such occasion would prove to me that when you want something bad enough, you can become very resourceful.

Through my travels around the country, I get chances to fish with some of the best anglers, and I always enjoy the chance to learn something new. While in Missouri, I went fishing with an angler who is nationally known through his own television show.

Many of the bass boys who fish professionally down south think we yankee fishermen are affected by the winters. I don't even want to mention this angler's name, but he thought it was a great privilege for me to have the opportunity to fish with him. Boy, did I want to fish his shorts off! The more I fished with him, the more I wanted to defend my ability as a Yankee to catch fish.

After three hours of rather slow fishing, I mentioned that all of our fish came just as our lures hit the water and that I had seen several fish following the lures. This observation didn't seem to affect my southern partner, so I adjusted my technique slightly and used the "stop-go" method of spinnerbaiting which I had never used before. I then reasoned that if they were striking as the baits hit the water, the fluttering of the spinners just before they started to move was getting the bass to strike., so I made a series of short stops in my retrieve (about twelve pauses per cast) just to see if I could turn some of those followers into hooked fish.

Nine straight bass later, my southern partner had a little more respect for this yankee angler. And after filling him in on how I had adjusted to the conditions I had come upon, he became a completely different person. He actually seemed like a nice guy!

This is one of many experiences that can be encountered when you experiment with your retrieve.

Brush Bombing

This is one method of fishing a spinnerbait that is used by many of the hard-core tournament anglers. This particular method of fishing is not easy. In fact, it is rather nerve-racking. Some lakes are better suited to this method than others because of the availability of thick shallow water cover for the bass to hide in.

The philosophy used in fishing spinnerbaits in this way is really very simple: bass will never stray far from their home. Their home could be a hole in a stump, an open pocket under a clump of reeds, or a post on a boat dock. Remember, bass like "things," and if you can place your casts within inches of these visual targets, you will catch fish. On the other hand, if your casts are not within a few inches of the "target area" then you are just wasting time. This is why you will then quickly reel in your spinnerbait and fire it in at another target.

Casting accuracy has never been more important than now, when your ability with a rod and reel can directly affect your success.

Reed banks are a good example of an area for "brush bombing," but so are lily pads, boat docks, floating bogs, or even a rocky shoreline. First you position the boat an equal distance from the area you want to cast to. This will aid you in making more accurate casts time and time again as you work along. You should never let your boat stop moving as you cover an area. Your casts should be made to land within inches of the object you are casting at and be permitted to flutter slowly down for a second or two, depending on water depth. You can do this best with your rod tip up to help slow the dropping process. Fish the spinnerbait with a jigging motion for about two feet, then quickly retrieve the lure for another cast! This entire sequence should take no longer than eight or nine seconds. Remember to keep looking ahead as you retrieve your spinnerbait, to where you wish to cast for a second time. Ideally, you will want to cast slightly ahead of the boat with your casts spaced about ten feet apart. This type of rapid fire saturation of an area can mean a big decrease in the amount of time it takes to find and catch a pile of bass. Spinnerbaits are commonly used for this hard core way of fishing, but so are some other lures that we will be talking about later.

Modifying A Spinnerbait

The true versatility of this lure is shown in the way that it can be customized to match the right occasion. One of the easiest tips I could suggest would be to change blade size. This can be done to any spinnerbait on the market, but again the Lund Buzz Bullet is a real favorite. This lure has a

Spinnerbaits come in many different sizes and designs. One option many anglers use is the changing of blades. A spinnerbait with a clip that attaches to the blade makes it possible to quickly change blade sizes.

small snap that you can quickly attach to any sized blade that you wish. The larger the blade, the slower you will be able to fish it, but the harder it will be to pull through the water. Smaller spinners are often preferred on gin clear lakes where too much flash can scare a bass away.

Not every spinnerbait on the market can be easily modified. Some manufacturers use extremely thin wire to support the spinner and, because of this, cannot handle larger blades. A fine wire on a spinnerbait can be an advantage in some cases, especially if you are fishing your spinner very slowly. At higher speeds this type of spinnerbait will run on its side.

Often when a lure is traveling past a clump of weeds or behind a stump, the bass is not in a position to grab the bait correctly. This will mean a very obvious strike, but a missed fish. To help solve this problem, anglers commonly use trailer hooks to increase the odds of the bass being hooked.

Every time I think about trailer hooks, I remember the time I was fishing on Horse Lake in central Wisconsin.

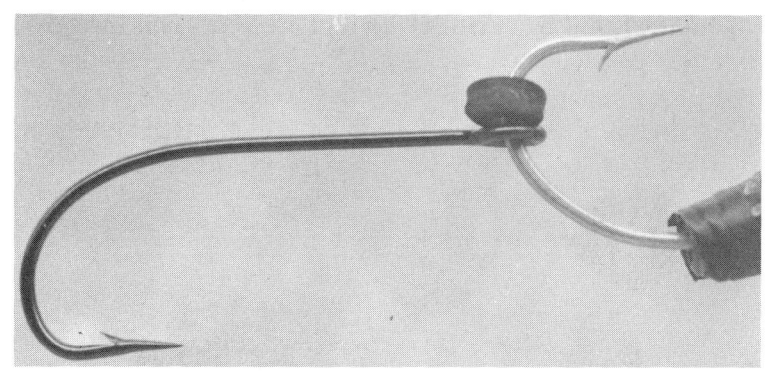

Trailer hooks are often added to spinnerbaits to give them extra hooking power. Note that the trailer in this case is turned opposite from the main hook. This gives great hooking power when fishing over deeper weeds, but can be a problem in shallow weeds. Also note the rubber disk that was stamped from an old innertube. This disk keeps the trailer from falling off while casting or while fighting a big bass.

This small lake was full of big bass, but exactly how big, I will never know. Early in the day a northern pike bit off my 1/4 ounce Buzz Bullet that I had rigged with a trailer hook. In the excitement, I just grabbed another spinnerbait from the bottom of my boat and began casting again. Suddenly, as I began to lift the spinnerbait out of the water for another cast, the hugh head of a bass came out of the murky waters below. It happened almost in slow motion as this bucketmouth inhaled my spinner right before my eyes! Dropping my rod tip, I let the fish swim off just a second and then tried to set the hooks. The bass had bit down so hard on the spinnerbait that the spinner was pressed against the hook. There was no way the single hook on the spinnerbait was going to hook that bass and with a toss of her head, the tangled mess flew back in my face. How big of a fish was it? Well, three casts later I took a bass over five pounds and I lifted it into the boat thinking that it was only a two pounder!

Trailer hooks can also come in handy if you are out after really big bass. If you take a look at the mouth of a really big bass, you can see just how much room there is to grab and spit a bait out.

By looking at the photo of trailer hooks, you can see that these are very special hooks that have eyes large enough to be threaded over the main hook on your spinnerbait. A

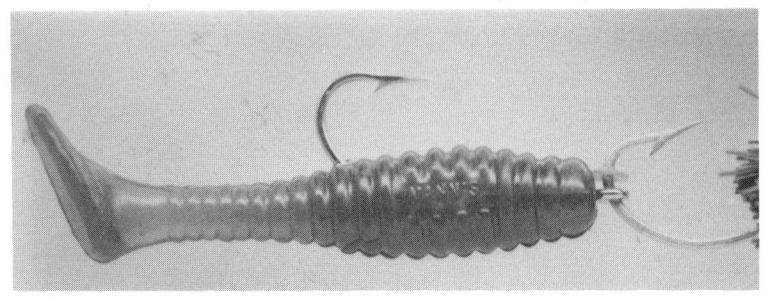

This trailer hook rig is set up with a rubber grub added behind a spinnerbait for extra appeal. Note the plastic disk that is used to hold the trailer hook in place. A paper punch was used to stamp this disk from a plastic coffee can lid.

keeper is a must to prevent your hook from flying off while casting or during battle with a big fish.

As you might imagine, tournament anglers will never fish a spinnerbait without a trailer hook. Anytime a bass grabs at their lure, it could cost big bucks if they miss it. On the other hand, in some very weedy areas the use of a trailer hook can be more of a hassle than it's worth. When a spinnerbait is drawn over a log or a clump of weeds it often rolls onto its side and the trailer hook becomes lodged on the object.

Another trick that many anglers use on spinnerbaits is the addition of a rubber worm or grub to the main hook. This little trick does two things for your bass fishing. First, the extra hunk of rubber increases water resistance. This will make it possible to fish the bait even slower and higher than before. Second, you will be able to make the bait look larger in the water. Many anglers believe that big bait draws big fish. I really don't believe that larger baits can produce as consistently as smaller baits. Except for in the fall, when bass will grab larger lures, the addition of a rubber grub or worm is completely optional.

The art of spinnerbaiting is one that is developed with time and practice. Like with any of the lures that we have talked about, the more time you spend fishing them, the more you will understand their effectiveness.

SPOON FISHING FOR BASS

In your arsenal of lures for attack, you have already learned about two of the most effective ways to take shallow water bass. Topwater lures are ideal for casting at targets such as open pockets in the weeds. Spinnerbaits are ideal when you want to cover a lot of shallow water in a hurry. To fill in the gap between topwater lures and spinnerbaits we have the family of spoons.

Often anglers in our weedy North Country lakes will find that the weeds form an umbrella on the surface to give shade and protection for the bass that freely swim beneath. The surface may be solid weeds, but four or five feet of open water may exist under the blanket of weeds. If you were in perfect casting stride, you might be able to drop your topwater lure into a small opening. After fishing several pockets like this you may get a frustrated. The bass could be scattered among thousands of pockets in the forest of weeds below. The perfect choice would be the use of a spoon to skim across the tops of the weeds and over those open areas that may be holding bass.

Spoon fishing has received a bad reputation over the years as a bait that gets strikes, but seldom hooks the bass. I remember fishing with one angler on the Mississippi River near La Crosse, Wisconsin. This skilled angler would use a spoon to draw bass from heavy cover. He sincerely believed that a spoon was such a poor hooking lure that he removed the hooks from his spoons. He would cast a hookless spoon deep into the thick cover and retrieve it quickly back to the boat. His trick was to get a bass to grab at the bait and to keep the bait moving so that the bass would follow the lure out to an open area in the weeds where he could cast a topwater plug to catch it on!

I had seen him do this several times in one day and became a firm believer in what I now refer to as "the one-two punch". This means that you simply get the attention of the bass with one bait, and catch him with another.

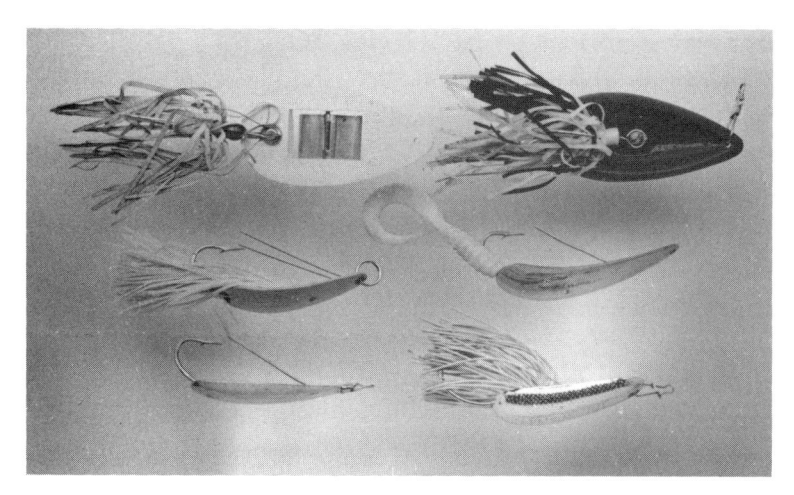

Super slop spoons come in many different weights and sizes. The Weed Walker (top left) sputters along the surface. The Moss Boss (top right) simply floats high in the water and is good only in very thick cover. The Timber King spoon (middle left), the Millers spoon (middle right), the Johnson Silver Minnow (bottom left), and the Talkin' Spoon (bottom right) all have the ability to be fluttered and dropped into pockets in the weeds. A spoon of any type can be productive if the bait is properly matched to the water that you will be fishing.

It has been an unwritten rule among spoon fishermen to always have more than one rod rigged and ready for action. Water boiling behind a spoon is a sure sign of an aggressive bass. Your goal is to cast a topwater lure within two feet of the boil in less than ten seconds after the fish is located. A bass can easily spook itself or loose interest in your offering if you miss the mark or wait too long to cast. My old river friend wouldn't even bother to retrieve the spoon all the way to the boat once the bass reached open water. He fired in his topwater lure immediately.

The one-two punch combination is commonly used by anglers fishing as a team in money competition. This means that one bass fisherman uses a spoon to attract the strikes, while the other is ready to cast to the subsiding boil with a topwater lure.

For years I believed that spoons were poor hookers, and

because of this had stayed away from using them to any real extent. One day, about five years later, I was fishing with a young lady friend of mine who wanted to learn how to fish lily pads for bass. I told her about the poor hooking ability of spoons in such situations and that it would be best to use a topwater lure such as Super Frog. I began to describe to her how important it was to not set the hooks when the strike was seen, but rather to wait for about two seconds after the boil before setting the hooks. As I was describing this method to her I began to think. Why don't I fish a spoon with the same guidelines and see what happens?

By keeping my rod tip high, I began to experiment with my hooksetting methods. The first bass was small and this little guy really busted the water to grab my spoon. Instead of trying to set the hooks, I dropped my rod tip and waited for about three seconds. I then reared back to set the hooks and to my surprise, I had the little guy hooked! I repeated the process several times that day and I NEVER missed a fish!

Spoon fishing is very exciting in many ways, because the strikes are very visible. The main problem with fishing a spoon is that the lure is constantly moving towards you. This enables you to set the hooks at the very sight of a strike. Like with topwater lures, the swirl you see is the fish coming to the bait, not the fish leaving with it. Eight out of ten times the bait is pulled away from the hungry bass. When a strike occurs, you will instinctively want to set the hooks. This natural reaction is the biggest problem with spoon fishing.

I have been refining my spoon fishing techniques in recent years since spoons have been included in my arsenal of attack. The simple key to the success of spoon fishing, like with topwater lures is knowing when to set the hooks! One of my major improvements in catching bass has been from the use of a seven foot, very stiff rod called a "Flippin' Stik". This long, powerful rod makes it possible to cast a country mile, and it can give you unheard of power in setting the hooks on a bass in heavy cover.

Using any line under twenty pound test can result in a lot of broken lines. With all the line damaging objects you can run into in shallow water, plus the everyday wear on the line, weak spots may occur. Heavy line is just added insurance for hooking and landing those big bass. Plus, you must set the drag on your reel as tight as possible to keep the head of the bass from burrowing into the heavy weeds below.

Several years ago I wrote a story called "Super Slop Bassin". It basically described how many of the big bass live all summer in the thickest weeds on a lake. When anglers complain about water skiers and other traffic on a lake, it's time to head for the thickest weedbeds you can find.

The procedure for fishing "super slop" is to use a heavy casting outfit and to cast your spoons as deep into the "junk" as possible. Keep your rod tip up and the spoon moving quickly across the surface. Your goal is to simply cover as many pockets and unique areas in the weedbed as possible. If a fish is found with a spoon and you are unable to hook it, then you should be prepared to drop a weedless topwater bait into the area within seconds.

Spoons come in many different styles, shapes, and materials. The material the spoon is made from is not nearly as important as its total weight and its ability to flutter slowly to the bottom. One plastic spoon, made by the Heddon company, is called the Moss Boss. This lightweight piece of plastic, shaped like a spoon, rides very high on the water and is perfect in the thickest of weeds. Unfortunately, this version of a spoon has no flutter or special action other than its ability to run over the tops of very thick weeds.

The old reliable Johnson Silver Minnow has been around for many years. This original bassin' spoon runs much deeper in the weeds than the Moss Boss and the Silver Minnow also has a very sexy fluttering drop as well. In areas of thick and then sparse weeds, the Silver Minnow would be a better choice than the Moss Boss because it becomes more versatile in open water.

The best dropping spoons I have used are the family of Timber King Spoons from Strike King Lures. These spoons have an excellent weight for casting, yet can be wobbled slowly into the pockets in the weeds. Through my travels around the country I have found that different areas prefer different types of bassin' spoons. One area may rely on the Miller Spoon, and another may favor the Pops Spoon. Having used them all at one time or another, I feel that it is important to get the feel of the drop and flutter of one or two spoon types to gain confidence and control in fishing them. I have not found any one spoon to be especially effective over another, only in the way in which it can be fished.

One of the most common ways to spice up your bassin' spoons is to add a piece of pork or a rubber grub to the main rear hook. As the spoon wobbles from side to side, the trailing piece of pork or rubber wiggles like crazy. Although pork rind is almost impossible to take off the hook and it stiffens in the hot sun in a matter of minutes, it is still your best choice of material to use as a trailer. Even with all the new advances in rubber products, nothing is as tough, yet as "sexy" in the water as pork rind strips.

Rubber grubs and other pork imitations simply do not hold up when you are constantly ripping a bait through heavy cover. Although rubber is cheaper to use and easier to take care of, the traditional strips of pork rind still have a definate place in your tackle box.

Constant adjustment to the metal weed guard is a must when you are fishing many of the metal spoons. This fine piece of wire plays a very important role in your ability to bring the spoon through heavy cover. Not having the weed

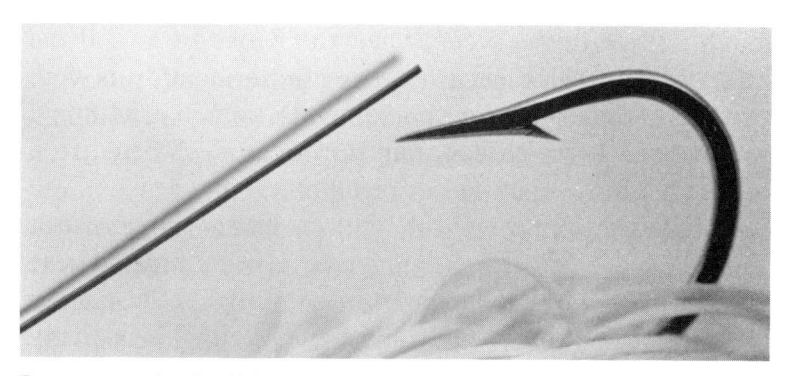

Be sure to check all lures that have weedguards. It pays to glance down at the lure after each cast to make sure that the wire or plastic arm extends slightly beyond the point of the hook.

guard set properly could be the reason for missing that trophy bass of a lifetime. Take a close look at the photo that shows you the proper distances to pre-set your weed guards. After each fish, and after each cast, you should glance at the spoon to make sure that the wire is bent to the proper position.

Spoon fishing for bass is coming on strong as the newly rediscovered method for catching bass in areas that many fishermen typically stayed away from. To the modern-day bass fisherman, the addition of spoons is definately a smart move. Bass anglers today must start looking beyond the hype of magazine advertising for solid advice in improving their fishing. A simple thing like fishing a spoon can be the difference between having just another average season and a great one.

Review of Shallow Water Tactics

With the wide variety of ways to use each family of lures, I find it very hard to decide on how to approach the problem of lure selection and presentation. Many of the lures I have already written about can be used in shallow, deep, or waters in-between. Although several other lure types can be fished in shallow water with special modifications, they are the exception rather than the rule. We will, of course, discuss those methods as we begin to talk about other areas that may hold a big pile of bass. Shallow water fishing, for the most part, is one of the most reliable ways to find bass. One proven method for increasing the total number of bass you catch is to be aware of what I call "visual structure". As you approach an area, you must select a lure type to match the occasion. In ultra heavy cover, you should use a spoon to cover water. In areas where you have a lot of open pockets, you may want to use a topwater lure. If you are fishing in areas of thick weeds that are just below the surface, the spinnerbait will let you cover water quickly and effectively.

The use of polarized sunglasses is a very important edge in your ability to visually spot the targets you wish to cast at. Keep your boat moving as you cast. Shallow water bass are the aggressive fish on the lake, so there is no need to drop anchor after one fish is caught. There are thousands of places where bass can hide along a shoreline. Your key to consistent success is to cover water, discovering which areas and lures the bass like the best.

CHAPTER FOUR
IN-BETWEEN TACTICS FOR BASS FISHING

The expression of "in-between", I know, is rather strange. But I felt it was the best phrase to describe where we are going to fish for bass next.

Fishermen often say, "The bass are shallow or deep OR somewhere in-between!" This expression is right on the money when it comes to finding bass and selecting lures to match the occasion. The depth ranges I speak of here will vary from lake to lake depending on weed growth and water clarity. With many lakes, the area of "in-between" water is very small. It is best described as that area where thick surface weeds end and the steep break to deep water begins. Some may call it "fishing a flat" or classify "in-between" waters as depths of five to ten feet. It is very hard to put exact depths on where you should fish on ALL waters. That is why you must be able to identify the water you will be fishing to help you better evaluate your needs.

The family of lures you can use effectively in this middle ground is quite different than many lures you might have used in shallow water. On the other hand, some lures such as the spinnerbait, can be adapted quite well to deeper water. Lets take a closer look at what lures can be used to fish the "in-between" areas on your lake.

Spinnerbaits On The Flats

Nearly all of the methods of fishing a spinnerbait I have talked about for shallow water fishing hold true now as well. The key in spinnerbait fishing is the current mood of the bass. If the bass are swimming high in the weeds, you have a better chance of appealing to them with a spinnerbait than you would if they were lying tight to the bottom. Spinnerbaits are effective in many lakes with long stems of weeds growing almost to the surface. Any other free swimming lure might get tangled in the stalks of weeds, but the almost weedless spinnerbait runs right through them.

The use of trailer hooks is very important when you expect your bass to be coming from under the bait to grab it. Since you are not in super heavy cover, there should be no problem with the use of trailer hooks.

Larger blades on spinnerbaits tend to slow the lure down, increasing the lures vibrations and visibility. On many lakes on which you can see down five or six feet, the larger blade on a spinnerbait will do wonders to "call up" a big bass. You can also cover water more easily and quickly with a heavier 3/8 or 1/2 ounce spinnerbaits.

The family of in-line spinners, such as the Mepps and Blue Fox Vibrax spinners, becomes very effective at this depth range too. Unfortunately many of these spinners have treble hooks behind the blades. These openly exposed hooks can make for tough going in heavy weeds.

Bass on Crankbaits

For many years, anglers were using hand carved pieces of wood called "plugs" for catching bass. The name "plug" simply comes from the plug of wood they used to make the lure. Fishing with plugs was a dying sport until the late seventies when anglers once more discovered the effectiveness of plug fishing. Lures such as the River Runt, Mudbug, and Pikie Minnow lead the way to a new fishing fad, "CRANKBAITING". The actual use of the word "plug" has gone by the wayside because the manufacturers wanted to breathe new life into the artificial lure business.

During the first few years of the crankbait boom, every manufacturer was coming out with a better-than-ever line of plugs, or as they are called now, crankbaits. Some had a realistic photo-like finish of a real sunfish or crappie painted on them. These baits sure did look great, and the amount of attention given to these lures was just as great. Within two years the boom was over and many manufacturers couldn't give the lures away!

The downfall of the crankbait business was no reflection on how well these baits could catch fish. Limits of huge

The use of plugs or crankbaits are top producers for smallmouth and largemouth. (left to right) Normark "Fat Rap", Mann's "Deep Pig", Rebel "Deep Wee R", Bagley's "Small Fry", and the Bomber "Model A".

bass have been taken on them. It was probably oversaturation of the market more than anything that brought their downfall. Now, the crankbait business is strong once more and people have been going crazy over the SHAD RAP. This classy looking lure is manufactured in Finland by the folks who make Rapala lures. Shad Rap mania was like the Cabbage Patch kid craze, with one lure selling for up to twenty dollars, or renting for a fifty dollar deposit!

As with most fads, it was more hype than anything. The Shad Rap is just one type of crankbait on the market today. There are currently a dozen manufacturers of lures which look nearly identical to the Shad Rap, and will probably catch you just as many fish. In fishing, there is no such thing as a guaranteed fish catcher or miracle lure for hauling in all the bass of your dreams. Crankbait fishing is just a way of fishing a certain situation when it arises. Time and time again I stress to the folks who attend my seminars to match the bait to the right conditions for success.

Crankbait fishing obviously can be more effective on one lake than another because of water clarity, bottom content, the time of year, and the attitude of the bass.

I can remember writing a story about how rock edges and points are fantastic for smallmouth bass at dawn and dusk. I described how the change in light penetration, with the sun close to the horizon, triggers the bass into feeding. The very next week I traveled to Lake Vermillion, which is right on the southern edge of Minnesota's Boundary Waters Canoe Area. This lake is full of bass and I was eager to get started. During what I thought were "prime" fishing hours, I caught only a few small walleye. On this particular lake, the bass go absolutely crazy at ten o'clock in the morning and feed untill three in the afternoon!

I fished hard each morning and evening, but took only a few two pound bass during these hours over my four day visit. This was mid-July and the weather was sunny, hot, and calm. I had no reason to think we would wear off the bills on a dozen Rebel Wee-R crankbaits catching bass in three feet of water during mid-day, but we did!

Many factors that we are unaware of can greatly effect the willingness of bass to start feeding. I, for one, never realized that the insect hatch was the triggering factor that got all of the bass in Lake Vermillion to go crazy. Every year since then, I have traveled to this great smallmouth lake to take advantage of this vacationers' dream. To be able to party all night, sleep late, and still be able to catch fifty smallmouth bass per day sure is paradise!

The crankbait family comes in many different shapes and sizes. Each style has its own particular action and running depth. The photo you see showing different styles of crankbaits is only a small sampling of the lures the avid bass angler has to choose from. Each year the choices get harder and harder to make.

For the "in-between" areas, the choice of crankbaits is limited to either super-shallow running cranks, shallow running cranks, or deep diving cranks. Your fourth choice could be the super-deep diving crankbaits, but we can really only use these types of baits for the deep water tactics we will talk about later.

The super-shallow running cranks are lures with no real bill or spoon shape on the nose of the bait. The Cordell Spot, Water Gator, Sonics and, especially, the Bayou Boogie are members of this effective crankbait group. The lack of a pronounced bill gives these cranks the action of a very rapid vibration. These baits by themselves would sink like a rock, but when you retrieve them very quickly they run just below the surface.

These super-shallow running cranks are great in shallow waters that have a thick blanket of weeds along the bottom. In many of the same waters where you might fish a spinnerbait, the super-shallow crankbaits can be used. Since these baits have treble hooks, they may have to be ripped through the weeds to prevent getting bogged down.

Your rod tip should be kept up while retrieving these baits, and your reeling pace should be almost as fast as you can turn the handle. With all crankbaits, the rod tip can play a very important role in your ability to control lure running depth.

This group of shallow running crankbaits has very much the same body shape as its deeper diving counterparts. The major difference is the size of the lip on the nose of the lure. The common rule is to take a look at the length of the body on the lure, and if the bill is 1/4 or less the total length of the lure it is a shallow runner.

The depth of a shallow running crankbait can be expected to be in the two to four foot range. Anglers who fish with crankbaits a great deal know how critical line size and lure speed can be in getting to the desired depth. It may seem like a trivial matter, but even the slightest increase in line diameter can affect your lure's maximum depth. A shallow running lure may be able to reach five feet with four pound

LINE BOW CREATED BY WATER RESISTANCE

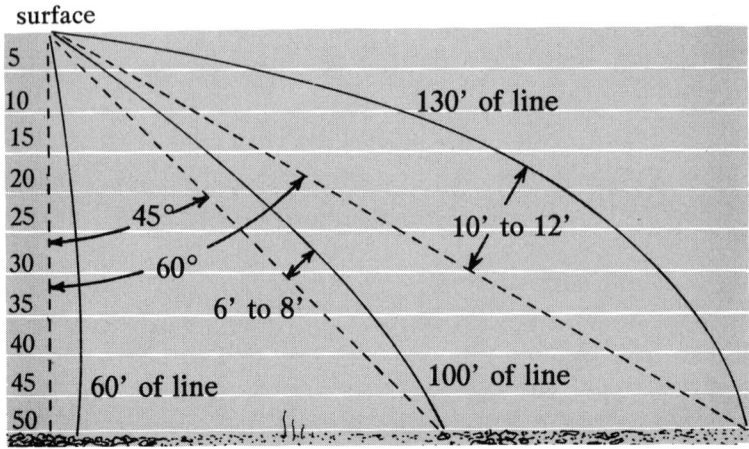

surface

depth		
5		
10		130' of line
15		
20		
25	45°	10' to 12'
30	60°	
35	6' to 8'	
40		
45	60' of line	100' of line
50		

As any lure or bait is pulled through the water, a constant force is put on the line. This resistance forms a bow in the line which is another form of slack line. This extra amount of slack can hurt your hooksetting power and decrease your sensitivity in detecting the bottom or a strike. The thicker the line diameter, the more resistance the water will put on it. Water resistance can also act like a parachute to prohibit some lures from reaching the bottom.

test line, but will never get any deeper than three feet with twelve pound test.

As a crankbait is pulled through the water the lure swims down out of sight. If you were to travel to a local swimming pool to learn just what does go on under the water, you would be shocked. Nearly all of the crankbaits on the market are designed to be fished very slowly to obtain maximum depth. Once you get the bait moving towards you, it may take up to ten feet for the lure to even get close to the maximum running depth. Speed compounds the problem of getting and keeping a crankbait down. Once the lure is moving at its maximum depth, any increase in speed will make the lure run shallower.

As with all crankbaits, the angle of your rod can play a major role in how deep the bait will run. A high rod tip keeps the lure high, a low tip can make a lure run up to three feet deeper with a normal cast.

The "in-between" areas on a lake often consist of a very

weedy bottom that you will want to keep your baits running just above. If the bass are holding tight to the bottom, the longer your baits are near the bottom, the better your chances of finding and catching a bass. One tip which I often share with anglers is the fast-slow method of getting a crankbait moving. Once a cast is made you will reel up the slack and get the bait moving towards you as quickly as possible. This means you should quickly turn the reel handle about five or six times to make the bait dig down. Once the lure has disappeared out of sight, you must slow your retrieve to a normal pace.

Deep running crankbaits are identified by having a long protruding lip of about 1/3 the total length of the lure. The family of deep diving lures is rather misleading. In pool side tests conducted on 50 of the leading crankbaits sold, very few were able to reach their stated running depth. On the package it might say that this double-deep diving lure is effective down to fifteen feet. In tests, this same lure never got any deeper than four feet!

It may not be a bad idea to get together with some friends and see for yourself just how deep some crankbaits really run. Here a group of avid bass anglers try every crankbait they own. They are checking the running depth of each crankbait so they have a better idea of what goes on when they start fishing.

It was obvious after the tests were made that the manufacturers had been using a different system of rating the depths that their baits would run. In the pool tests, we used ten pound test Stren line and made what we considered to be "average" casts. The only way many "deep diving" crankbaits could live up to their advertising would be to troll at long range with two pound test line.

I thought at first I should wave some consumer alert flag on crankbaits. After all, I really didn't consider five feet as being deep. But that was the average depth range of a "deep diving" crankbait. As a fisherman, this means a lot in my choice of choosing a lure to match the occasion.

From a versatility standpoint, deep diving crankbaits are a better choice for the angler to use. In the proper hands, a deep diving crankbait can be fished slowly above the weedy bottom, bumped along the bottom, or ripped through the stalks of weeds. The Razorback from Mann's Tackle Company is my first choice in deep diving crankbaits with the Rebel Deep Wee-R a close second.

The super-deep diving crankbaits are real killers to cast and retrieve all day long. These baits are designed to head

The front lip on a crankbait will determine just how deep it will run in the water. On the left we have lures with metal bills. These are often the deepest divers of all. The long plastic lip on some crankbaits means it can dive to great depths. The smaller the lip, or even the lack of one like on the lure at the far right, will mean a shallow runner. Knowing how deep your crankbait will run is critical to selecting the proper lure for the water you are to fish.

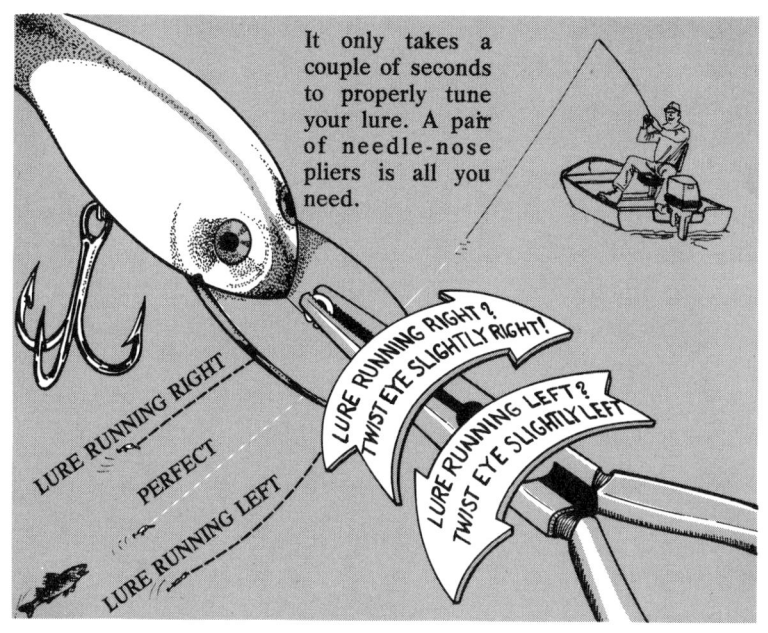

Plugs or "crankbaits" often need a little fine-tuning to insure they will run straight. It is wise to tune every lure before you start fishing to make sure it is giving you the proper action.

straight for the bottom. Lures with names such as Hellbender and Mudbug make up this last category. These bottom-loving lures often have metal lips instead of plastic. Metal seems to be a better material to use if you want the bait to really get down and dig. We'll be talking more about the use of super-deep divers later in the book.

The use of noise makers or rattlers in a crankbait is one of the many features you may choose from. A rattler can be important in both clear and stained waters for attracting the strike of a bass. The inventors of the first noise chambers in a bait claimed that it was easier for the bass to zero in on your lure. This extra awareness could only result in more fish. The makers of wood and solid foam crankbaits say that they scare off more fish than they attract.

I have found no definite answers to either claim in my years of fishing with crankbaits. For reasons of confidence, more than anything, I prefer to use lures with rattles rather than without. However, I do believe that you can go a little too far at times with the rattles in some crankbaits. Some have a single bead that gives a soft rattling noise. Others shake like a rattle snake and are so loud you can hear them in the water twenty feet away!

With any crankbait, you should always tie directly to the lure. Some lures already come with a very small "o" ring to tie your line to. With other crankbaits, you will need to use a small clip to attach the lure to without restricting the wob-

Connecting your line to a crankbait can be done in many different ways. If an "o" ring is already on your lure, you can tie direct. With other baits you will need to use either a small snap swivel or just a plain snap to let your crankbaits wiggle freely.

ble action of the lure. Some lures demand that you use a snap, otherwise they won't work at all! The use of a plain snap in contrast to a snap swivel is another important tip. You do not want any more additional hardware on the line than is absolutely necessary. The color of your snap really isn't as important as many might think, but to play it safe use black snaps in very clear water.

Obviously, line size can play a very big role in the performance of your lures. It would be nice to say that for all crankbaiting you should use ten pound test, like we used in our pool testing. From a more practical point of view, twelve and fourteen pound test lines are better choices. The everyday use of monofilament in and around weeds can stress even the heavy lines. Bass taken from the "in-between" areas of your lake are likely going to dive for the bottom, and they can be hard to turn. Heavier line has some disadvantages, but the advantages far outweigh them.

Plastic Worm Fishing

The family of artificial, plastic, or rubber worms is by far one of the most versatile. I have failed to mention them to any extent up to this point because they can be used in almost any situation with the right modifications.

The nearby photo shows just a small sampling of the variety of worms on the market today. Tomorrow there could be just as many new styles to choose from.

For a shallow water application, the styles that are almost all "curl" tails or resemble lizards drive bass crazy. Using them with a single split-shot and rigged in a weedless manner, you can fish in only a few inches of water.

For deeper water applications, use a heavier sinker in front of the worm. These are often cone shaped in design to help guide the worm around weeds and other obstruction. The more you wish the worm to stay on the bottom, the less "curl" you will want on the tail.

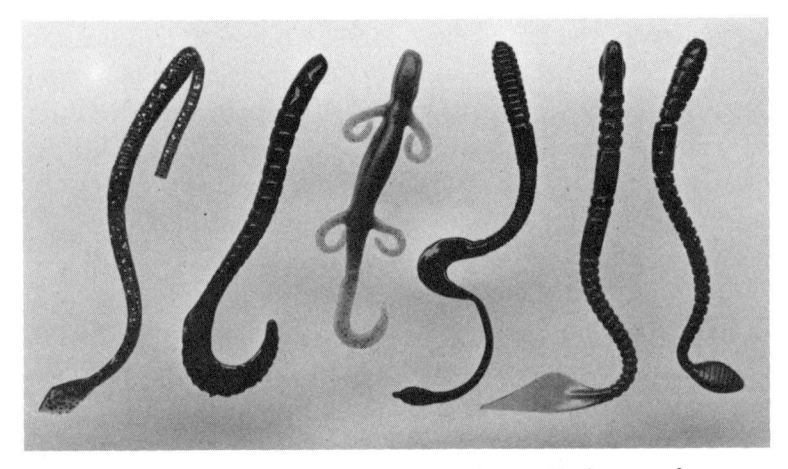

Plastic, or rubber worms, as they are often called, come in many different shapes and styles. Few North Country bass are taken on worms longer than six inches. Worms with a large curl tail permit a slower drop. Worms with a straight tail tend to be the best choice when bouncing along the bottom because their tails float higher. Salamander worms are one of the best baits for early season bass.

Rigging a worm can be done in several ways. As the situations arise, you will be able to select the hook style you like the best.

The open hook is the simplest way of rigging a rubber worm. Bare jig heads, like those commonly used in walleye fishing, are perfect. 1/8 ounce jigs are the most popular size to use. Of course, the depth of water you fish has a great deal to do with the jig size. When fishing an open jig hook, the worm must be pushed all the way up to the jig head for best results. If for any reason the worm has slid down the hook, it must be straightened out as soon as possible.

Jig head shape can play a big role in your ability to get the worm through that occasional weed without hanging up. A stand-up or wedge shape to the jig head makes it easy to rip through weeds, and it tends to have more of a swimming action as it drops. The popular round-headed jigs will work just fine for most anglers, but they tend to foul easily.

A relatively new jig head design, called an umbrella jig, drops as well as a round-headed jig, but it permits the hook and worm to stand almost straight up when it rests on the bottom.

Obviously, you cannot use a rigging method like this in areas that are too thick with weeds. Many skilled worm fishermen like to fish an open hook by swimming the worm over the tops of the weeds. The big advantage in fishing this rig is the ease with which the hooks can be set. In many cases the bass almost hooks itself. This means that the angler can enjoy the use of light tackle to fish and fight out a bass.

A weedless hook attached to a wire weed guard was one of the first ways in which a rubber worm was used. In very shallow water, the weedless hook rig is extremely effective when rigged in a "weightless" manner. Other than that, the weed guard tends to be more of a catching spot for moss than for bass. This is by far the least popular way of rigging a worm.

The Texas rigged worm is one of the most popular ways to present a rubber worm in heavy cover. With the hook buried into the body of the worm, we will have almost no problem at getting through or around cover and brush. The photos show the step-by-step way to rig a worm Texas style.

The single downfall of this weedless rig is getting the hook set into the tough jaw of the bass. The only way to do it correctly is to bear down and try to "rip their lips off!" No matter what I say in print, it will never stress the importance enough of a powerful hookset in this type of bass fishing.

In all of worm fishing, either fishing slowly on the bottom or swimming the worm above it, the bass gobbles down a worm the same way. It may seem hard to visualize bass inhaling a seven inch worm in a fraction of a second, but they can! In theory, the worm fisherman could set the

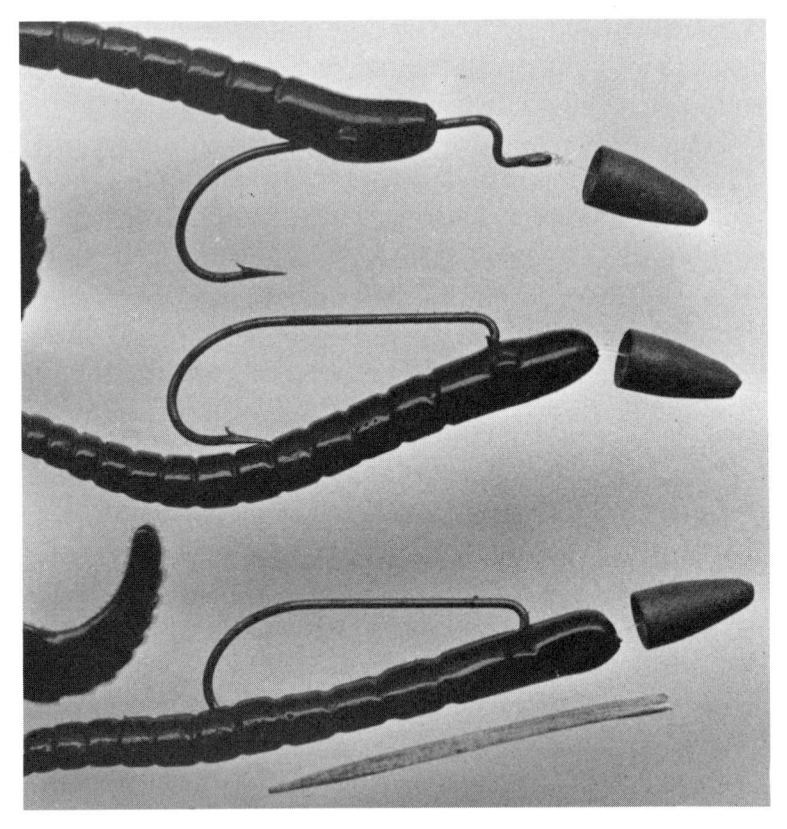

The Texas rigged worm is made by first using a special hook and sinker combination. A 2/0 hook is the most popular for this type of fishing. The worm is first threaded on the hook, as shown, from top to bottom. A toothpick is then inserted into the sinker hole with the line to keep it from slipping away from the worm. You can see that this rig is extremely weedless, but it is critical to set the hooks very hard to pull them through the worm and into the jaw of a bass.

hooks on a bass as soon as the fish is felt. The big problem with this is that unless the bass is in a good position to be hooked, a strong hookset may be a waste of time.

A good angle for hooksetting is critical to your odds of landing that bass. As with top water baits and spoon fishing, waiting for the bass to swim off is critical to the success of the hookset. In worm fishing, the strike is felt and not necessarily seen. Watching your line where it makes contact with the water is the secret. Your line is far more sensitive than any fancy rod. By becoming a "line watcher", you will see your strikes long before you feel them.

Once a bass grabs your worm, don't be in a hurry to set the hooks. If you are fishing directly over the fish, you can set the hooks right away. If the bass hits at a full cast, you had best wait until you have some idea of which direction the fish is moving.

One of the first areas in which I had ever used a Texas rigged worm was on Lake Minnetonka, which is a series of channel connected lakes just west of Minneapolis. The boat channels connecting one lake to another are some of many great fishing areas on this lake. These man made ledges often hold schools of bass, and if you catch them right, you can take a fish on every cast.

On this lake you need to keep your boat away from the channel walls. Your goal is to keep your bait right down next to the metal walls. When a bass picks up your worm, he will quickly run away from the others in the school. This move is often made to deeper water to get away from the others. This is often straight towards the boat. When I first experienced this type of fishing, I missed three out of four fish because I never took the time to visualize what was going on under the water before I set the hooks. Once I knew that the bass was trying to keep the bait away from their buddies, I knew that he was not going to let go of his prize right away. It is common to let the bass swim with the bait for eight or ten seconds before the right angle is reached for a hookset! This very hard act of patience can pay off with an almost 100% success ratio on hooking bass. Not only did I catch more of the bass that hit, but I also didn't spook the school when I let the bass get away from the others. This made it possible to catch several fish while casting to the almost identical spot time and time again.

Getting overly excited is easy to do, and only after you

have a few fish under your belt will you begin to master the skills and patience a good worm fisherman must posses.

The action that can be given to a rubber worm will vary with the day. An easy hopping action along the bottom will drive most bass crazy. Many good walleye fishermen, who are familiar with jig fishing, can make a quick transition to bottom fishing a worm. When the bottom is clean, it is often a good idea to let the worm lay motionless on the bottom to entice even the biggest of bass. Bass have always shown the preference of grabbing a falling worm. Smallmouth especially love to ambush a grub jig just before it hits the bottom. With any of the worm rigging methods I have described, the falling or dropping action of a worm is where 80% of your strikes will occur.

All winter long worm fishermen dream of that very obvious "ting" in the line as the worm drops to the bottom. Often the best way to fish a worm is to let it fall to the bottom, then reel quickly for about two seconds, and let it fall back to the bottom. This is very similar to "swimming" a worm. The only major difference is that you will need to let the bait drop all the way to the bottom.

Fishing the "in-between" waters with a worm is a very slow process. In many ways, worm fishing should only be done when you wish to take a closer look at an area. The ideal tool for covering water in this region is the crankbait. Once a prime area is located, and one or maybe two fish have been caught, then it is time to break out the worms. Some anglers fish worms all the time, but if you're learning a new lake this tedious way of fishing can waste a lot of valuable time.

Making the proper lure selection for the area you wish to fish now starts to get a bit complicated. Many lures that we fish in shallow waters can be adjusted to fish deeper waters. The rubber worm can be modified to fish anyplace, but in the amount of water it can cover it is like a top water

This seven pound pre-spawn female was taken on a rubber lizard, one of the author's favorite springtime baits. Spring bass are often very fickle, but a rubber lizard or salamander has proven to be one of the baits a big bass just can't ignore.

lure. With top water lures, you are firing your casts to an open pocket or area that you feel could hold a bass. Once you have fished the area, it is best to simply reel the lure in and try again in another area. Worms are also very much a "spot" bait where you pick a target or area you really want to check out. Granted the suspense is there but unless you know the bass are down there, you could be wasting valuable time.

In my younger years, before turning "pro", I ran a fishing tackle department for five years. In that time I was able to find out why some lures always seemed to sell well. The answer was very simple. The easier the lure was to fish, the better it sold. Although I was actively involved in tournament bass fishing at the time, and plastic worm fishing was the hot method, I couldn't sell a worm. Every year I would end up putting my inventory on sale because the average guy didn't want to take the time to master fishing them. Worm fishing is by far the most challenging way to land a bass, but that doesn't mean it is meant for the tournament fisherman only.

Getting started in worm fishing should really begin with the open jig hook rig we have talked about. The jig and worm rig is a very effective way to fish a worm as well. The biggest problem many worm fishermen have is gettig a strong hookset. With the jig and worm combination you greatly increase your ability to set the hooks, and at the same time increase your confidence in this type of bait.

CHAPTER FIVE
DEEP WATER BASSIN'

For years the schools of bass which held in deep water were left untapped. Anglers would beat the shoreline and maybe the edge of a thick weedbed, but that was about it. With the invention of the electronic depth finders, a whole new frontier in fishing has been opened.

Moving away from using any visual forms of structure took some getting use to. North Country anglers at first adapted walleye fishing methods to bass fishing. The always productive jig and minnow combination scored big on smallmouth and largemouth bass.

To clarify what is meant by the word "deep", it is important that we analyze the lake we plan to fish. Deep water is basically the outside edge of the weeds. On some lakes, the weedline may grow down to fifteen feet. A heavily stained lake may have a weed edge ending at only five or six feet. The amount of sunlight that can penetrate into the water is in direct proportion to weed growth.

Today, the use of electronic depth finders is critical to your ability to position the boat. As you motor your boat from deep to shallow, watch the dial on your flasher. As the signal gets more shallow take note of a series of small spikes which start flashing just above the bottom signal. These small spikes of light mean there are weeds along the bottom. Note what depth you were at when they started to appear. This is how you find the outside edge of the weeds.

You have a choice of positioning your boat on top of the weed edge or just to the outside of it. Keeping an eye on the depth finder at all times is critical to keeping your boat in the proper position. Just as with an unusual shape along the shoreline, any variations in the shape of the bottom contour can form a bassin' hot spot.

The lures you select to fish these areas obviously must run fairly close to the bottom. We have already discussed many of the lure types, but not how they should be used.

Crankbaits, for example, are extremely effective on deep water bass. I would boldly say that to catch just the sheer numbers of bass, crankbait fishing would be the answer. The deep diving cranks with lips at least 1/3 the length of the lure should be used. At best, these baits can get down to six or seven feet. This depends on the line size you use and how far you can cast. Many of the super deep divers such as the Hellbender, Bomber, and Mudbug, are built with metal lips instead of plastic. The Bill Norman Tackle Company also makes a line of super deep divers called the Deep "N". These baits have plastic lips almost as long as the body of the bait itself.

Although very productive on deep water bass, I will be the first to admit that it is the most physical of all the baits. While conducting some tests on the maximum diving depths of many of the leading crankbaits, I was tired after only a few casts with these super deep divers. This is of course not their fault, they have to push a lot of water to swim down eight to ten feet on just an average cast.

From a fishing standpoint, it may not be a bad idea to switch lure types you are using in deep water so you will not tire as easily.

Anglers are advised to try to keep their baits as tight to the weed edge and the bottom as possible. On some lakes you may have to keep your rod tip up to walk the bait over the tops of the weeds, and then as deeper water nears, drop the rod tip to let the bait swim deeper into the water. Your rod tip has a lot to do with the maximum running depth of any crankbait.

One of the big bassin' boys down south won a tournament using a method that he calls "kneelin' and reelin'". With this variation of fishing a crankbait, he kneels along the side of the boat while a special seven foot rod is submerged almost to the reel handle. This method of sticking your rod tip under water permits the lures to run even deeper.

It is critical to remember that turning the handle on your reel as fast as you can is no guarantee that your bait is reaching its maximum depth potential. Often just an easy reeling pace will get the desired results.

The proper tuning of a super deep diving crankbait is very critical. Please refer back to the diagram on the tuning of a crankbait on page 83.

Deep water bassin' is often one of the best times to use a plastic worm. By letting the bait drop straight to the bottom, you can fish the entire bottom area all the way to the boat. Deep water wormin' is time consuming and you must move your boat ever so slowly as you fish along the shoreline. Even a little breeze can make for some very challenging worm fishing, because you must be aware of the lightest of pick up.

The jig and worm or jig and grub rig is by far the #1

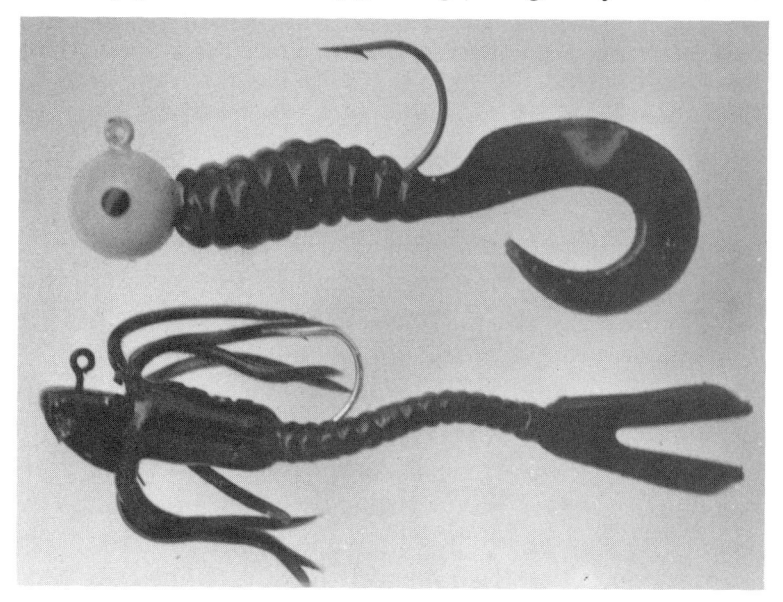

A twister type grub jig and the Lund Backswimmer jig are two great choices for the smallmouth angler. These bite size baits are what smallmouth seem to prefer. The size of jig you use will be in direct proportion to the water depth you are fishing.

choice for deep water fishing, unless there is a stringy kind of weed that makes fishing an open hooked rig more difficult. The deeper the water, the more critical it is you use a heavier weight ahead of the worm or grub. The jig and worm rig permits the use of a lighter rod, and the use of eight pound test is often more than enough. This lighter line

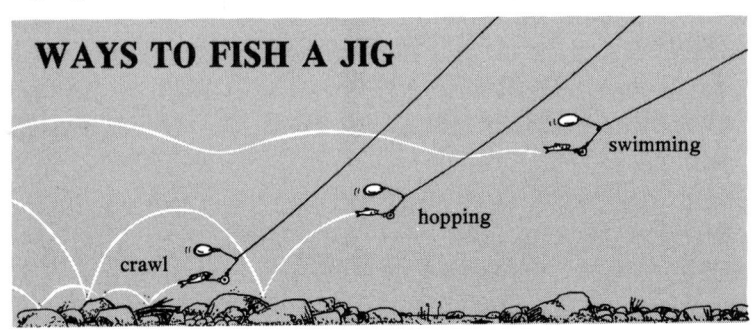

WAYS TO FISH A JIG

swimming

hopping

crawl

Jig fishing for largemouth or smallmouth can be very productive. The secret to success is finding out if the bass like baits being crawled, hopped or retrieved steadily above the bottom. Many times it is a wise idea to add a spinner to the jig to slow down the drop and make it easier to fish over weeds and snags.

will also permit you to use a lighter weight jig head in deeper water. You will want to use the lightest jig hook you can for one very good reason. The slow dropping action of a jig and worm drives bass crazy! Unfortunately if any wind is blowing, you may have to use a heavier jig head to keep better control of the bait.

The third option you have for deep water fishing is the use of the deadly "REAPER WORM". The Reaper is a rather strange looking, eel-like rubber worm. These baits are one of the best ways to quickly cover a deep area for bass. The way this bait is fished is a lot faster and more erratic than a standard jig and worm rig. They are both rigged basically the same, with the rubber bodies threaded on the hooks, but Reaper fishing involves a larger jig head. Some of the best have a wedge shaped head to help them to cut through any weeds it may run into.

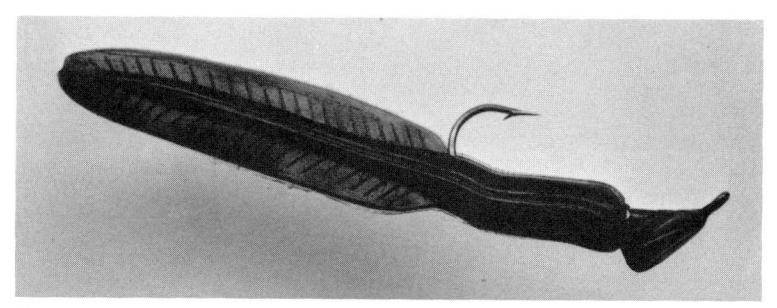

The Reaper worm is one of the most productive lures to fish down steep drops or through thick weeds found in deep water. Although it doesn't have a wiggle action, it does dart and swim from side to side and bass have a hard time refusing it.

To fish a Reaper you will need a stout rod with at least ten pound test line. Your casts should be up towards shallow water. Let the Reaper drop to the bottom while watching the line for any sign of a strike. By keeping the rod tip at waist level, you simply reel as fast as you can for about five turns. If you feel any resistance at all, yank back on the rod as hard as you can to rip the bait clear. You then stop cranking and permit the bait to fall once again. With your rod tip again at waist level, you repeat the process until you are to the boat. You will notice that as you reach deeper water the bait will require more time to reach the bottom. This ripping and dropping action is one of the best ways to get a bass to strike.

Another deadly way to score on big bass is the use of the "jig & pig". Basically a jig & pig is just a jig with rubber or bucktail added to give it sex appeal. To the jig is often added some sort of extra action. It is often a chunk of pork rind or plastic imitation with a curly tail. This lure combination has a reputation for appealing to the big bass. It looks great in the water too, with the bushy skirt and the curly tail giving life to the bait as it drops through the water.

The procedure for fishing a Jig & Pig is basically the same as that of a Reaper worm. The only difference is that a pig drops four times slower. You simply spend more time

The jig and pig lure combination is considered by many to be one of the best big fish baits you could use. The traditional pork rind is on the left, and the new plastic versions are on the right. By adding one of these to the back of a feather, rubber, or bucktail jig, you will slow the drop rate considerably. The bass have a hard time resisting it!

letting the bait drop to the bottom. The bass will always strike as the bait is dropping, so it is critical you have pressure on the line at all times to detect a strike. As soon as a fish hits, set the hooks as hard as you can. When you fish a slow dropping bait like a jig & pig, there is a lot of slack line in the water you may not even be aware of. This is one of the reasons you must keep you rod tip below waist level to insure a powerful hookset. One of the other major problems is that when a bass is deep below you and you must set the hooks on her, the only place the hooks will find a home is in the bony upper jaw of the bass. The hooks on a jig & pig is often quite large and very strong. This is good for hooking power, but make sure the hook is razor sharp before you make your first cast.

Deep water bassin' is one opportunity to hit some real gold mines on your favorite lake. No other area in a lake will big bass be found in such numbers. Anglers finding these areas often can take fish on every cast until the school is spooked or they have caught them all! Fishing deep water areas though, takes a lot of time and patience.

I must again stress the importance of boat control at all times when you are fishing deep water. It is not easy to spend the day fishing an imaginary piece of structure on the bottom. You must learn to mentally draw a picture of the bottom contours as you fish along. A marker buoy is not a bad idea to use when you're fishing far from shore. If I were asked what was more important in the success of deep water fishing, the lure I used or boat control, boat control would win hands down!

CHAPTER SIX

BASSIN' RODS AND REELS

With the lures that I have already talked about, it is extremely important that the correct fishing outfit be used. One of the great things about bass fishing is that anglers can use a wide variety of tackle. Because of this, the tackle manufacturers seem to cater to bass fishermen before all others. If a new method or style of bass fishing comes to light, WAM! A new line of custom rods appears for just that purpose.

I personally think that this is great for the industry and for the fishermen who want to enjoy their sport to the fullest. The problem with this method of marketing a product is that it confuses the everyday fisherman. Only a small percentage of anglers, under very limited situations, will ever be able to use many of the products developed for bass fishing.

What I am really trying to get across is that you might have heard of some super-duper rod material, for example, which is so sensitive you can feel an ant walk across the guides! The actual use of this rod is actually no better or worse than one that you might pay fifty dollars less for.

Matching your equipment is very important in obtaining what I call a "balanced" outfit. There are, of course, many different combinations of rods and reels that work very well together. First a rod must be selected, and then the reel. To finish off a well balanced outfit, the proper line must be chosen to complement both the rod and the reel.

In selecting rods, there are literally thousands of different types to choose from. I will be the first to admit that I have problems selecting the types of rods I like to use. Most manufacturers try to simplify the task of selecting a rod by rating each blank. Located on the shaft of the rod, just above the handle, you will find this information.

Unfortunately, there is no standard in the industry as to

what a "medium" action rod is. One rod may be designed to handle lures up to one ounce while another can only handle lures up to 1/2 ounce. Fishing rods are a lot like golf clubs in that you must match the rod you select to the conditions at the moment. This is done by matching the correct lure to the correct conditions first, and then putting it on the right outfit for the job. If I wanted to fish an area of lily pads, I might use a Johnson spoon that weights 1/2 ounce.

The leaps of a smallmouth can send chills down the back of even the most skilled angler. There isn't too much you can do to control the jump of a bass. If you have time, and see that your line is headed towards the surface, you might want to put a little less pressure on the bass and put your rod tip into the water. Some fish you will be able to turn, while others will jump several times no matter what you do.

Knowing the weight of the lure is important in your ability to cast the lure, but you must also remember where the lure is to be fished. In heavy cover such as lily pads a bait casting outfit designed to handle line sizes up to twenty pounds, and a rod that is just as strong, is very important. Trying to fish a spoon with ten pound test on a light action spinning rod can only result in a broken line or rod as the fish runs into heavy cover.

There is no place for light action rods when fishing bass in heavy cover. However, these types of rods CAN be used for bass fishing. Often when the bass are on the edge of heavy cover the use of a jig and worm, or even a small crankbait on light tackle, can be very effective. Here the angler can get more enjoyment out of fishing with lighter tackle.

The type of rod material used in the making of a rod has no real bearing on how or where this rod should be used. The action of a rod is what determines where it should be used. The angler today has several different rod materials to choose from. Graphite, fiberglass, boron, and kevilar make up the major categories. The big trend in the industry today is to blend these different materials together. Fiberglass as a rod material is very durable, and when blended in the right ways with graphite you have a super light and durable rod. The cost of many rods with graphite has come down dramatically over the past five years and the quality of the rods has improved. No matter which type of rod I recommend, there are always some people who like to spend a lot of money on a rod, while others are looking for the best price. Graphite rods are still the best value for the money and for their performance. Although you could spend $100 more on a boron/kevilar rod blend, it will not seem much different than a $39 graphite!

For casting accuracy, a short rod is a good idea. Many of my favorite rods are not more than 5'3" long. Some of these rods can be very stiff, while others are quite soft. Be sure to get one which can handle both the line and the lure sizes you will need the most. In bait casting, I prefer to use rods which can handle up to 25 pound test line and lures to at least 1 ounce. This is what I would typically look for if I was using spinnerbaits on a baitcasting outfit.

For throwing crankbaits, I like to stay with longer rods.

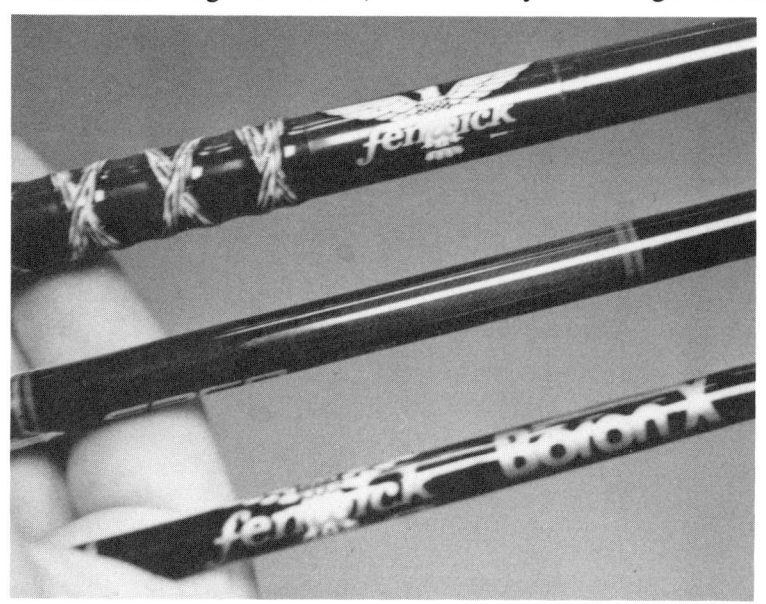

These rod shafts are all made from different materials but are designed to handle the same lure and line sizes. Note the fiberglass blank on top has the largest diameter. The graphite rod in the middle is noticeably smaller in diameter than the fiberglass rod. The boron rod on the bottom is only slightly smaller in diameter than the graphite blank. The total weight of the rod shaft will also be affected by the materials in the rod.

Often a crankbait is difficult to throw because it is lightweight. A six to seven foot rod with an action that can handle lures to 3/4 of an ounce is often perfect.

For spinning tackle, I like to have good line control and casting accuracy, so my rods are again short. I very seldom use a spinning rod over five and a half feet. For worm fishing with spinning tackle I use two different rods. One is the lightweight 5'3" rod that can handle lures to 3/4 ounce.

The other I use for Texas rigged worms. This rod is 5'6" long and has a very stout action. It is rated for lures up to one ounce. I need the extra power to insure a good hookset with a Texas rigged worm.

For fun and some real sport with smallmouth, I often bring along a short, light action spinning rod that is designed to handle lures up to 3/8 ounce. Rigged with only four pound test, this outfit makes landing even a small bass a great challenge.

I also find a big need for what I call a special purpose rod. The "Flippin' Stik", is a seven and a half foot rod. This powerful rod can easily catapult a three pound bass right out of the water when you set the hooks! This rod is great for flippin' and for fishing a spoon in very heavy cover. It is rigged with at least 25 pound test line for best results.

These six rod styles cover about 95% of all the bass fishing you will ever do. You also have the option of fly fishing for bass as well. Here many anglers use a rod over eight feet in length and use fly lines with a rating of eight or more. These bassin' fly rods need to be more powerful than what you would use for panfish or trout because the bass bugs that are often used can be very difficult to throw with light line weights. I have a special chapter later in the book dedicated to just fly fishing if you wish to learn more about this great method of fishing bass.

Reels

One of the most underrated portions of a balanced outfit is the selection of the proper sized reel for the rod and line that you will be using. Time and time again I have seen anglers with reels designed to handle a line up to twenty pound test and they have it spooled with four pound test! Putting a deep sea spinning reel on an ultra light rod defeats the purpose of the light action rod. I am always very critical of the balance on a outfit because of sensitivity. Many manufacturers jump up and down about how their rods have such superior sensitivity. The only problem is that most strikes are seen first, and not felt. Even an inexpensive rod can detect a bone jarring strike. In many cases the angler will feel only a slight increase in the weight of the lure. This ever so slight increase in weight is hard to detect if the rod has a heavy tip. The overall weight of the reel

A five pound smallmouth is a fish that will test the skills of any fisherman. You will not find another fish that can fight like a smallmouth. It has been said that, pound for pound, the smallmouth is the toughest fish that swims.

used to be a major problem, but today it is more important that you first have a reel designed to handle the size line you need. This is by far the most important factor in casting and fishing performance.

Within the family of reels, we have three basic groups: spincast, spinning, and bait cast. The spincast reels are the most simple to operate, with a single button on the top of the reel. You push the button and the line goes out. Turn the reel handle and the line comes back in. Anyone can learn to cast one of these outfits in a few seconds. These spincast reels are simple, but they do have some faults. By nature, they cannot retrieve line as fast as other reel types and they are not capable of working very well with heavy line.

The spinning or open face reels are designed by nature to cast light weight lures and to work with light lines. Spinning reels have been very popular with anglers who like to fish with light tackle. When lures are to be fished very slowly and carefully, no other type of fishing outfit can give you such control and sensitivity. A bass fisherman can often get by with not spending more than thirty dollars for a very

Here are some of the more popular reels used by fishermen today. The spincast reel on the left is the most simple to operate. The open face spinning reels are great for light line. The newest styles of bait casting reels are great for heavy lures and lines.

good spinning reel.

Bait casting reels are much more expensive than spinning reels. In fact, sixty dollars is just the bottom range of what you might expect to pay. This family of reels has come a long way since the old direct-drive level wind reel my father owned. With a reputation for backlashes (I refer to them as professional over-runs), these reels are now not nearly as bad as many anglers remember.

As a youngster I worked at my casting day and night. It took me nearly two weeks to master using a bait casting outfit. Today I can teach non-fishermen to use the reel in a matter of minutes! The ultra smooth drag and high speed gears makes this reel the workhorse of the bass fisherman. Designed by nature to work with heavy lines, this is the only type of reel that many anglers can use in heavy cover. The gearing system makes it possible to retrieve lures that are hard to pull through the water with ease.

One of the things to look for in a reel is to make sure that it is smooth. Any extra vibration in the reel can numb your sensitivity. Look for the lightest reel of a particular size. All reels will break down at one time or another, so be sure that you are aware of the company's service policy. If possible, try your reel on the rod you plan to fish with and see how well it feels. Don't be afraid to ask the salesman for his input. Often the guys behind the counter are avid anglers and have some good suggestions.

In fly fishing, the reel is of little importance at all. The major purpose of a fly reel is to simply hold line. A single action fly reel that is large enough to handle an #8 weight line or better is all that is necessary.

Fishing Lines and Knots

Today's fisherman has come a long way since horse hair was used for fishing line. Improvements and breakthroughs in manufacturing have brought us to use synthetic materials such as nylon. By far the most popular type of fishing line on the market is the family of monofilament lines. When I say "family", I mean that there are many different blends of nylon used in making fishing line today.

The DuPont company was the first to blaze the trail with monofilament line. They now manufacture Stren, the #1 selling line in America. Over the years the composition of Stren fishing lines has changed dramatically. Constant breakthroughs in the blending of nylons served to improve the line even more. The folks at Stren looked to design a line with just the right amount of stretch, limpness, and toughness. Anglers must remember that although monofilament lines of today are extremely good, they do have their problems. What the chemists need to do is blend into the line various properties that they wish to have. The only problem, is that there is always a compromise. The thinner the line you make, the more fragile it becomes. The tougher the line is, the more memory it has and it becomes hard to cast.

This is why there has been a great amount of rivalry among line manufacturers. One company may make the toughest line, but it lacks other properties that are also important such as line diameter and limpness. Many people like to use one make of line and stay with it. I recommend you always stay with a "premium" quality line. Stren is a great choice for the bass fisherman.

Your fishing line is unfortunately not always without fault. During the course of a day you may encounter boat docks, rocks and logs, and of course tree limbs. This is why a tough line must be used in bass fishing. You will be spending most of your time in and around objects that bass like to hide behind. The section of the book that is dedicated to fishing knots will cover many of the more practical knots you will use. Your knots will always be put to the full test several times during the day. It pays to take some time now to practice your knots to be sure that you have them down BEFORE you tie on that five dollar lure.

Stay alert for any nicks and scratches in the line. The area just above your lure is often nicked while casting and can weaken your line dramatically. This is good advice that many people fail to realize until it is too late.

Change your lines regularly. It is just good insurance to keep fresh line on your reels. You may not need to remove all the line each time you wish to add new line. The use of "backing" is a money saving idea that can come in handy. By filling your reels half full with dacron or old fashioned black nylon line, you reduce the capacity of the spool. In bass fishing, you will never need more than fifty yards of

By adding backing to your reels you will be able to replace the line that is used most often. This not only saves money because you only have to replace the last fifty or sixty yards of line, but it also means you can use fresher line at all times. This can be done with all types of reels. Braided dacron line works the best because it will not shrink or rot on the spool.

line on a reel at one time. Most reels can handle 200 yards of fresh line, but you will end up wasting 150 yards of it. This will be an added incentive for you to keep you reels full to capacity at all times as well. A full spool will make for longer casts and better retrieve ratios.

Line twists often come from the lure twisting the line as it drops or as it is pulled through the water. No make of line twists any easier than another. The way the line is fished controls the amount of line twist you will encounter. In the methods of bass fishing I talk about in this book, there is really no need to use swivels. The only lures that rotate completely around are the Dardevle-type spoons. Even with the famous Johnson Silver Minnow a swivel is not necessary because the bait does not revolve completely around. At best, a small snap is all that you will need.

You really can't prevent line twists before they happen, but you can correct the problem. When line twists become too much of a problem, simply remove all of the hooks, snaps, and sinkers from your line. Begin to troll and feed out just the bare line. Water resistance will quickly grab the line and pull it off the spool. Once you feel that the twisted portion of the line is out, engage the reel and drag the bare line for about one minute. Once this is done, simply reel in the line and the twists will be GONE!

When you are thinking about the size of line that you should use, remember to think of the areas you plan to fish the most. If you have one "heavy" outfit, be sure to keep at least twenty pound test on it. Most mid-range outfits should run with twelve or fourteen pound test line, and light outfits should run with eight.

Many fishermen ask me if bass can see your line and I respond with, "Yes, I think so." Then why not use the lightest, most invisible line for fishing? The answer is simple. I just don't believe that if bass see your line they will swim away from your lure. Many anglers believe that the fish actually follow the line down to the lure! I have seen it time and time again with panfish in my own pond. First they notice your line, and then they seem to follow it down until they find your worm.

Monofilament line is far from being the "perfect" line that all fishermen would like, but it is the best that we have to date. Anglers should also be aware of the environment they live in. Monofilament fishing line NEVER deteriorates in water. That means if you throw some tangled line in the water, it will still be there long after we're gone. Birds can get caught in it, and motors can be ruined by it. So keep our lakes cleaner and safer for everyone by disposing the line so it will never get into our lakes and rivers.

Fishing Knots

Learning to tie a good knot for fishing should be learned while at home, so you will not need to waste precious fishing time trying to master a new knot. Anglers should be able to tie their favorite knot in the dark as a good test. Fishermen will of course not need to learn all the various knots in this book, but each does have a special purpose that can come in handy if the occasion arises. (see diagrams)

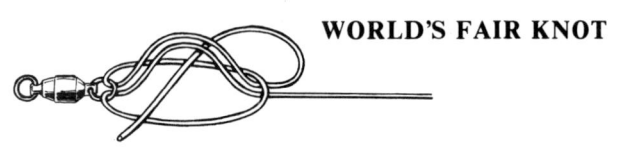

WORLD'S FAIR KNOT

A. Double a 6-inch length of line and pass the loop through the eye.
B. Bring the loop back next to the doubled line and grasp the doubled line through the loop.
C. Put the tag end through the new loop formed by the double line.

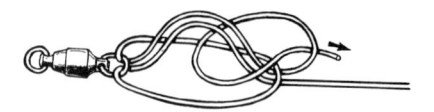

D. Bring the tag end back through the new loop created by step C.
E. Pull the tag end snug and slide knot up tight. Clip tag end.

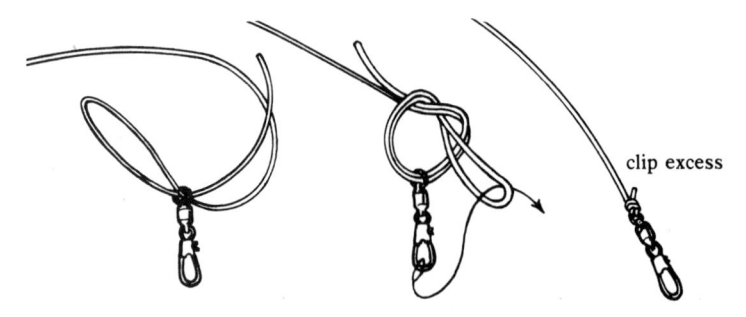

clip excess

The PALOMAR KNOT is considered to be one of the strongest knots known to tie on terminal tackle. The double wrap of mono insures a strong connection and a strength factor of 85 to 95 percent of the original line strength when tied properly.

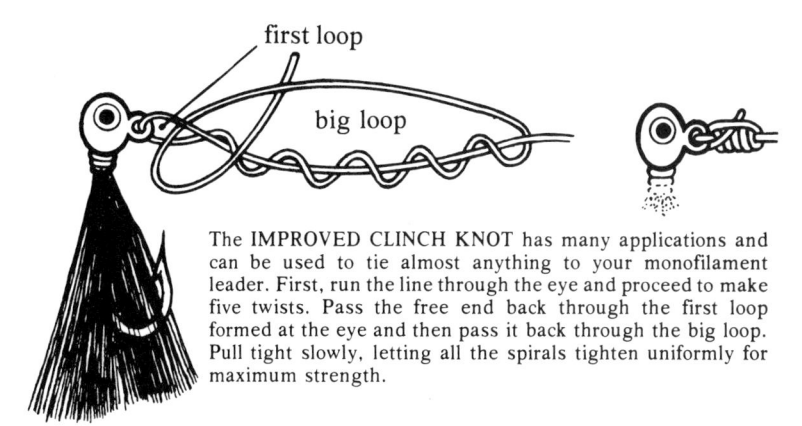

first loop

big loop

The IMPROVED CLINCH KNOT has many applications and can be used to tie almost anything to your monofilament leader. First, run the line through the eye and proceed to make five twists. Pass the free end back through the first loop formed at the eye and then pass it back through the big loop. Pull tight slowly, letting all the spirals tighten uniformly for maximum strength.

Jansik Special

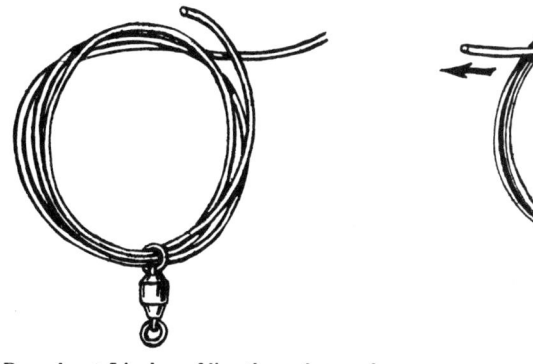

Run about 5 inches of line through eye of hook on lure; bring it around in a circle and run it through again.

Bend standing part of line around the two circles. Bring tag end around in a third circle and wrap it three times around the three parallel lines and draw tight.

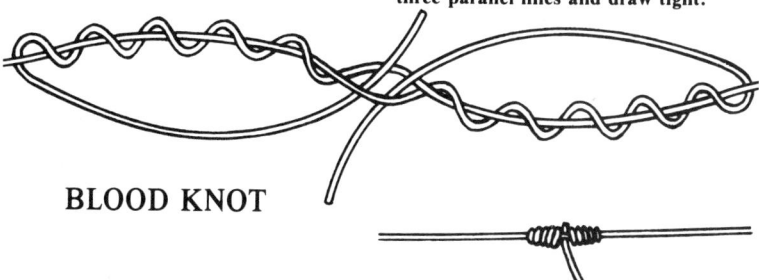

BLOOD KNOT

Want to join two pieces of line together? Use a BLOOD KNOT. When twisting, use five turns on each side, making sure they are in opposite rotations. When the knot is correctly formed as shown, pull it tight and clip off the excess.

Surgeon's Knot

This knot joins a leader to line just like the Blood Knot, though where lines vary in diameters.

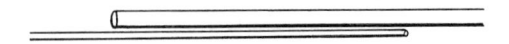

A. Lay line and leader parallel, overlapping 6 to 8 inches.

B. Treating the two like a single line, tie an overhand knot, pulling the entire leader through the loop.

C. Leaving loop of the overhand open, pull both tag end of line and leader through again.

D. Hold both lines and both ends to pull knot tight. Clip ends close to avoid foul-up in rod guides.

Albright Special

This knot is used for tying a light line to a heavy monofilament leader or a wire leader.

A. Double back a couple inches of the heavy line and insert about 10 inches of the light line through the loop in the heavy line.

B. Wrap the light line back over itself and over both strands of the heavy line. While doing this you are gripping the light line and both leader strands with the thumb and finger of your left hand, and winding with your right.

C. Make ten turns, then insert the end of the line back through the loop once more at the point of original entry.

D. Pull gently on both ends of heavy line sliding knot toward loop. Remove slack by pulling on standing and tag ends of light line. Pull both standing lines as tight as possible and clip off excess from both tag ends.

CHAPTER SEVEN

BOATS FOR BASS FISHING

They say you can tell the age of a boy, by the price of his toys. Well in bass fishing, there sure are a lot of big kids out there! Every season thousands of dollars are spent in the name of better bass fishing. In the tournament circuit, if you want to be a contender you MUST have at least an eight thousand dollar boat. It may sound rather strange, but this seems to be the case.

First off, boats don't catch fish! I have yet to see a boat land a single bass in competition or otherwise. People catch fish, and it's as simple as that. Boats are just devices to make you more efficient while you're out there fishing. Owning a boat that costs twelve thousand dollars is no guarantee the bass will be impressed. Even an inexpensive "belly boat", which is just an inner-tube you can sit inside, can be great fun for bassin'. Many of the smaller, more remote lakes in the North Country are inaccessible by regular fishing boats. Fishing from canoes is very common on the bog lakes of northern Minnesota and Wisconsin. There is nothing wrong with those of you who own a fancy metal-flake boat. These fancy toys are great fun. Heck, I own three myself, but it is not the boat that catches the bass its the people in it!

Some fishermen without boats keep telling themselves that they will be great AFTER they buy one of those fancy toys. Nothing could be farther from the truth! Needing a fancy boat to become a great bass fisherman is just an excuse.

A "fishable" boat is a great phrase to use to discribe a good fishing machine. What do we really mean by the term "bass boat"? I think if people saw a boat with a raised casting platform, electric motor on the bow, and nice carpeting,

The type of boat you are fishing from does not make you a great bass fisherman. On smaller lakes and farm ponds, the belly boat is a more practical choice with many anglers. The stable and comfortable innertube boat is one option many anglers use on those tough to reach lakes.

would be thinking "bass boat". Granted, these features can be adapted to nearly any type of fishing boat. That is just the point I am trying to make. You can easily customize an inexpensive aluminum or fiberglass boat to make your own "bass boat". Adding these very features to boats I have owned has been a lot of fun. It doesn't have to move at fifty miles an hour to be a true bass boat.

The natural lakes of the north are hundreds of times smaller than the reservoirs down south, and this is the problem with bass boats. The majority of those metal-flake jobs that are referred to as "rockets" are made for the southern reservoirs. The natural lakes we have are often just too small to realize any benefit from a boat that can travel at eighty miles per hour. Many of the southern boat companies are having problems marketing these rocket boats in the north. The ten thousand dollar price tags are in reach of only the true hard-core bass guys.

Sleek and stable, many of the newer hull designs make bass fishing as comfortable as possible. With an electric trolling motor mounted on the bow for easier maneuvering, these fancy boats are a true pleasure to fish from.

Many anglers have families and must think about fishing from a more practical point of view. For this reason, the trend in the north has been towards the smaller versions of the fancy bass boats, or even aluminum boats modified to look like bass boats on the inside.

Many of our northern lakes can get a little rough, and anglers feel that an aluminum boat with a big bow is safer than a sleek low riding bass boat. For this reason, the modified walleye boats have meant big business for the boat manufacturers. Many of the smaller lakes along the east coast have horse power restrictions and small boats are a way of life out there.

Except for a few larger lakes where tournaments are held, I feel the market for the super-high power boats is quite small. I have found this to be the case when trying to sell two of my boats at the same time last spring. In the ad I mentioned an aluminum boat with a 50 horse power motor and one of my rocket boats with only a 115 h.p. I received over fifty calls one Sunday afternoon for the aluminum boat and only ONE for the rocket.

One boat which I have fallen in love with is the Ranger 1600 series of boats. These scaled down fishing machines with 50 h.p. Mariner outboard on the back are the Cadillacs of fishing boats. This type of mini bass boat is quick, stable, and simply fantastic in big water, as I have been known to do a little walleye fishing from time to time.

The hull design you select with your boat has a great bearing on the performance of the boat. High performance boats are often referred to as being "pad" boats. This phrase describes a flat portion of the hull near the drain plug. At high speeds, this boat actually rides only on this "pad". This hull design is very quick, but often hard to control and hard to ride in any type of wind. The "V" hull boats or modified "V" hulls are designed to cut the water more

Speed is one advantage that many of the sleek bass boats have on their side. When every second counts, tournament anglers are looking for every edge they can get to put more fish in the boat. High performance boats can cost as much as fifteen thousand dollars.

and offer a drier, smoother ride in big water. Although slower out of the hole than a "pad" boat, the "V" hulls are by far a more desirable hull for fishing.

Boats with aluminum hulls are often not as sleek because they are not designed to travel as quickly through the water. The flat bottomed Jon boats are commonly used by river fishermen. These boats draft very little water and make it possible to get into areas that other boats can't even get near. Jon boats are a super choice for river fishing, but in lakes they become very wet in waves are are unsafe in

For shallow rivers, the Jon boats are the ideal choice for fishermen. As you can see, they are extremely stable and draft only a few inches of water.

Fishing from a canoe is popular on many shallow rivers. The aerial jumps of the smallmouth can make for some very exciting moments in a tipsy canoe. Be sure that a life jacket is worn at all times to insure a safe fishing trip.

truly big water.

Most aluminum boats are designed with "V" hulls and they cut through the water and big waves very well. One of the disadvantages of aluminum boats is that so much of the hull sits above the water. This can make boat control a real challenge in any kind of wind. With some practice and a lot of electrical power, you should be able to control the boat in any fishable situation. Of course, if the wind is blowing at thirty miles per hour, no boat can be controlled very well.

LIVE WELLS, This is one feature commonly found on the REAL bass boats. Basically, a live well is nothing more than a portable aquarium that is used to hold your bass. Although many boats have them built right into the design of the hull, a simple ice cooler can be quickly con-

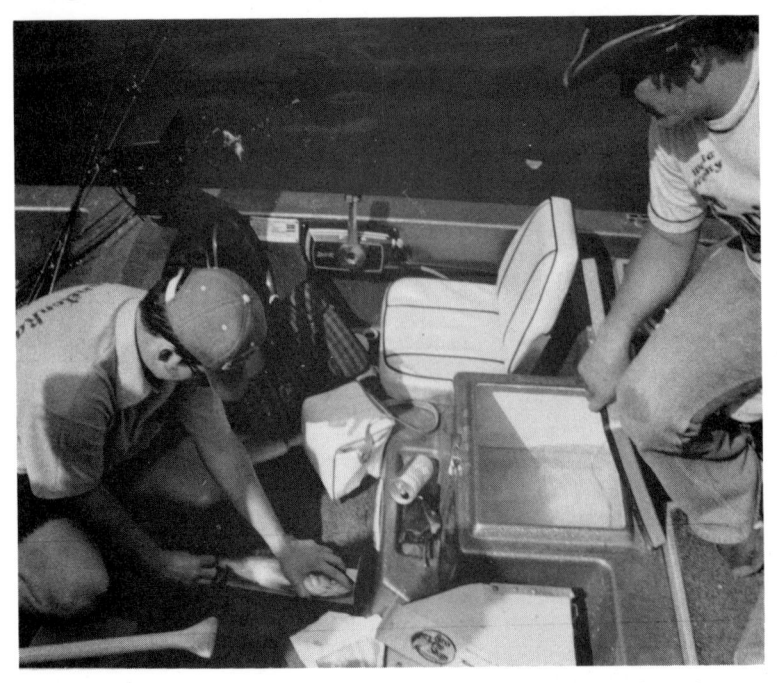

Live wells are often built right into the hulls of fancy bass boats. Many of the larger models have two or even three wells. Even on the hottest of days, a bass can be kept alive all day long and then released safely.

verted into a portable live well. This is done by adding a portable aeration system that runs off a twelve-volt battery system. This aeration system keeps the water well oxygenated for several bass to live in.

On those hot summer days it may be wise to add some ice to the live well. This reduces the bass's need of oxygen and keeps them lively. There are also several chemical additives that basically do the same thing for the bass. These chemicals, when added to the water, calm the bass down to reduce their need for oxygen. A product called "Catch Saver" is commonly used with tournament fishermen who are penalized if any of their fish die before they are weighed-in.

This boat was just a bare shell, but when a casting platform, rod rack, rear bench seat, live well, and a bow mounted electric motor are added you have a great fishing machine. Once you have reached your fishing area, this boat is just as comfortable to fish from as a ten thousand dollar boat.

OUTBOARD MOTORS The costs of today's outboards stresses the importance of good maintenance. Not too many people will spend three or four thousand dollars on a motor and not want it to last. Although you might be able to take a plain boat and jazz it up, there is only so much you can do with an outboard motor.

The owner's manual promotes the importance of a

Changing plugs along with other simple maintenance tasks is one way of getting better performance out of your motor as well as preventing the majority of on the water problems anglers may run into.

yearly tune-up with a regular changing of the spark plugs and lower unit fluid. Just like with cars, if you take care of them, they will take care of you. One of the great things about fishing boats is that the value of a boat and motor doesn't depreciate like with cars. You will often be able to use a boat for two or three years and sell it for exactly what you paid for it.

Making sure that your boat is properly matched with a motor is important if you like good performance. NEVER exceed the BIA rating for the size of outboard that the boat can handle. Besides being against the law, it isn't very safe.

Features such as a power tilt and trim are a wise idea if you like getting into the shallow regions of a lake without bogging down in the weeds and mud. It may cost five hundred dollars to install a power tilt and trim unit on your motor, but it is one of the best investments you could make in taking the work out of fishing.

Boat trailers are often overlooked and this can cause nothing but problems in the long run. Often a "package" deal comes with a great boat and motor, but a cheap trailer. This makes for tough launching and loading, along with poor support of the hull. Try to get the best possible trailer for that particular boat. For the high performance hulls, a carpeted bunk trailer is the only way to go. These trailers require enough water at the launch sight to be able to float the boat on and off. The bunks are needed to support the hull while trailering. The roller trailers are great for aluminum boats and make launching in only inches of water possible, but they can easily wear holes in fiberglass boats. A good trailer will cost nearly a thousand dollars, but will be well worth it.

There are many different boat and motor combinations to choose from. It would be foolish for me to try to list names. The key thing to remember about selecting a boat is to make sure it can offer some of the features I have mentioned. A well designed boat can give you years of angling pleasure and make the sport of bass fishing even more fun.

BASS FISHING ACCESSORIES

On your bass fishin' rig, there can be many gadgets that can make the time between strikes a little more fun. Some of these gadgets are almost essential, while others are just gimmicks.

ELECTRIC TROLLING MOTORS

This is one of those gadgets that the average bass fisherman would never be without. Your boat's weight and draft above the water controls which size motor you should have. You can never have too much power when you select an electric trolling motor. I always recommend the strongest motor that a manufacturer makes, unless it is going on to a very small aluminum boat. To avoid electrical problems, many of the newer 12 volt systems are gearing up with more power than ever before. Thirty-six pounds of thrust for a 12 volt motor is excellent and one of the motors offered by Minn Kota. Minn Kota motors are by far the largest sellers in the North Country, and they offer some of the nicest features in motors as well.

The use of 24 volt systems is a little more complicated when it comes to wiring and maintenance. On many of the larger boats, this is often the only way to offer enough power to move the boats along.

Mounting the motors on the bow of the boat is done for several reasons. The biggest is for better control of the boat in the wind and for the least amount of water resistance in moving the boat forward. On aluminum boats that have high bows it is critical to have extra long shafts on the motors. Otherwise, every time a wave comes by the prop will bob out of the water. An electric motor mounted on the stern will have to work much harder to push or pull the boat through the water, and it also makes boat control in any wind a real challenge.

Bow mounted electric trolling motors are very popular with bass and muskie anglers who do a lot of casting. Foot control models make it possible to maneuver the boat while keeping your hands free to cast. While mounted on the bow, these motors are able to pull the boat at a surprising rate without a sound.

A new feature on electric trolling motors is the weedless prop. This unique design makes it possible to run an electric motor through thick weeds without clogging up.

Consumers have the choice of selecting a motor that they can operate by hand or by foot controls. The big thing down south right now is the use of hand models that can be controlled with a kick from the operator. If the control cable that operates the foot control is broken, control of the boat is lost. To avoid the odds of this happening during competition, the hand operated models are big with the tournament boys.

I've been lucky, I guess, but because of the freedom of movement and better boat control found with the foot control models, they are by far my personal favorite. The newer models in the Minn Kota line have a super dependable cable system, and I, quite frankly, wouldn't be caught without one on my bow.

The batteries used for electric motors are extremely critical to the overall performance of the motors. First off, the deep cycle marine batteries with at least 105 amps of power should be used. These batteries are designed to take the constant strain of power loss all day long.

A fully charged battery should easily last all day. At every chance possible, a battery charger should be used to return the batteries to full charge. It has been my experience that when a drained battery goes without charging for very long, it shortens the life of the battery. Many anglers use two or even three batteries in their boats to insure enough power. One is used to start the motor, and two twelve-volt deep-cycle batteries are hooked up to the same twelve-volt system for days of extra power. Keep the acid level on all batteries up to par. The constant charging often causes a loss of water which can also shorten the life of a battery.

ELECTRONICS

In the world of bass fishing, the importance of "fish finders" or sonar units is extremely important. One of the key factors to deep water boat control is boat position. Without a depth finder, This would be simply impossible.

In recent years, the breakthrough in the electronics field has led to many great things for fishermen. One item which has changed very little in recent years is the "flasher." This type of sonar unit has a rotating bulb that flashes the

A flasher unit is by far the most important depth finding tool every fisherman should own. This particular unit has a special sun screen so that you can see the depth clearly even with a bright sun.

bottom signal. This unit is the depth finding device EVERY fisherman should own. It can be used on any boat and can be mounted so that it is possible to find the bottom at speeds of sixty miles per hour!

The way this gadget works is beyond my simple mind. A portion of the flasher called the transducer is placed in the water and the long cord is connected to the unit itself. A signal is sent through the transducer and it bounces off the bottom. The length of time it takes for the signal to reach the bottom and to bounce back up is recorded on the rotating dial. The flasher bulb lights up once on the calibrated

Transducers that send and receive the signals for the flashers and graphs should be installed in fiberglass boats in the back drain hole area. Silicone or epoxy should be used to make sure there is no air between the bottom of the transducer and the hull of the boat. This can be also done with some aluminum boats if used in shallow water such as rivers where mounting them on the outside of the hull could result in damage from rocks.

Aluminum boat owners will find that in order to get the strongest signals the transducer should be mounted on the outside of the hull. Note how the bottom face of the transducer is slightly below the hull of the boat to insure a good signal.

zero mark on the dial, and again at the depth of the water that you are in. If the bottom is hard, you may recieve what is called a "double echo." If the bottom is at fifteen feet, and you see another bottom reading at thirty feet, you know that the bottom is rocky or just very hard.

With a flasher, you can also identify weeds and even fish in some cases. Don't think for a second that this device is a "fish finder." Too many people think that these tools of fishing will solve all their fishless days. THEY WON'T! Take a good, hard look at the owner's manual to learn all of the features and workings of your individual unit. The manual will also show you how to mount the transducer so that you will be able to get a strong bottom signal no matter how fast you travel.

There are several quality brands to choose from, and you can expect to spend $150 to $250 on a flasher unit. When you do purchase a unit, be aware of warranties and service centers near your area. ALL units will break down from time to time and it often pays to buy a unit that can be serviced locally.

The next step in the gadgets for fishermen is the family of graph or chart recorders. Computer chips have made it possible to add features to these units that were never before possible. Basically, these chart recorders are the same as a flasher, except that the signal is much stronger and your signals are recorded on paper instead of a series of rapid flashes on a spinning dial. Although a big asset in fishing the Great Lakes for trout and salmon, and fun to play with for walleyes, the chart recorders, which can run from $400 to $800 are just a waste of money for bass fishermen.

I'm sure that I won't win many friends among companies who manufacturer chart recorders, but I want to be as straight with my readers as possible. You didn't buy this book to read commercials. You want to learn the real facts that can help your fishing and I hope I have done so.

WHAT'S HAPPENING DOWN THERE?

GRAPH RECORDER

Vertical school of baitfish

Horizontal school of baitfish

Single fish

FLASHER UNIT

What we think we're seeing

the real world

stationary boat

shortest distance to transducer

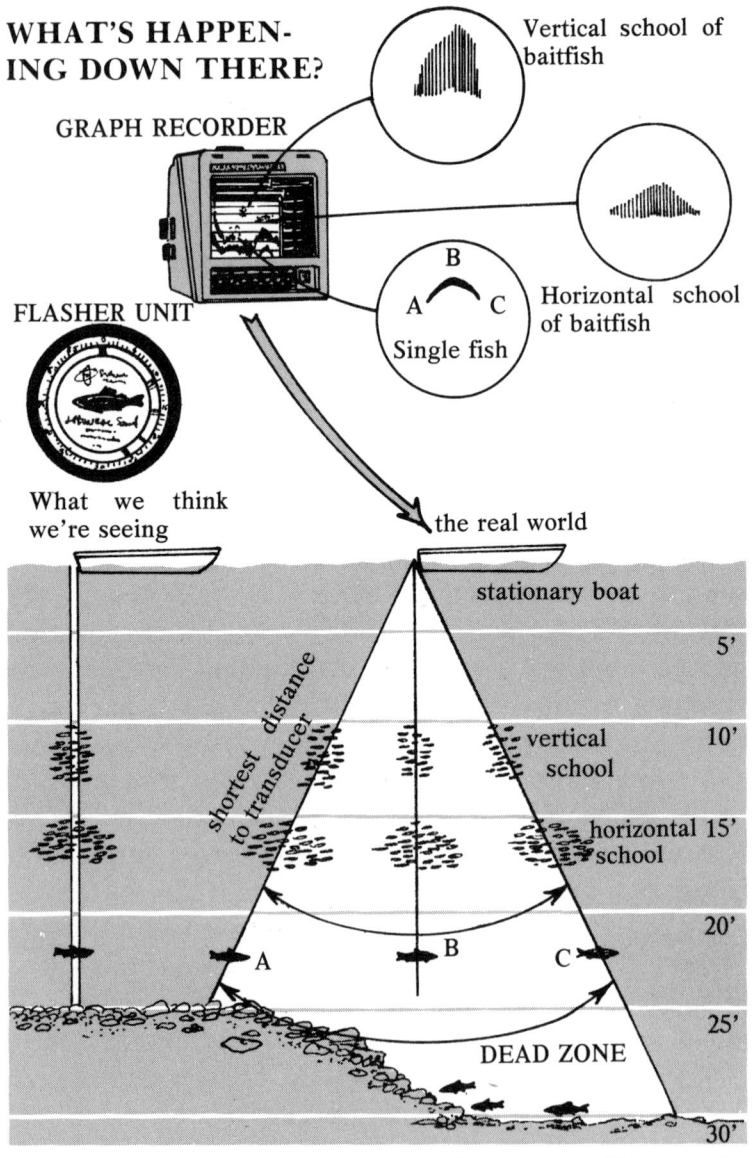

vertical school

horizontal school

DEAD ZONE

5'
10'
15'
20'
25'
30'

The flasher unit on the left gives you the same readings as the chart unit on the right, but in only a one dimensional view for a split second. The graph readings can show individual fish as hooks. They take this shape as the fish come closer to a direct position under the boat and then leave. Note the dead zone in the signal area created by the small ridge along the bottom. This problem is one of the reasons you can catch fish from an area where the graph shows none!

Here we have one of the most popular paper graph units. Now equipped with computer parts, these compact depth recording devices have come a long way in recent years and are very reliable.

One new twist to the chart recorder scene is the addition of the new T.V. screens. The new ones are coming out on the market this year for $300 or less, and they look great! Paper graphs cost an additional five or six bucks a roll for every eight hours of use. The T.V. screens never need paper, have no moving parts, and are completely waterproof. This looks like the trend of the future, and if the price stays down they can have a definate place in the bass fisherman's boat. The great thing about a chart recorder is that it gives you a visual picture of what is below. This can offer anglers a better mental picture of what is below. In bass fishing, though, much of your fishing is done in less than ten feet of water, so chart recorders are not necessary. As one veteran angler once put it, "I don't need a depth finder. Heck, if I can't touch bottom with my rod tip, I'm too deep!"

TEMPERATURE GAUGES

Seasonal changes in the north often play a big role in bass fishing activity. The use of temperature gauges in finding the warmest temperatures in the spring is as important as a depth finder! This is important on large lakes or backwater areas of rivers, where an isolated pocket of warm water may be hard to find. On smaller lakes the factors of warm and cold water may not be as severe, but they can definitely affect your success.

A digital temperature gauge is one device that can greatly affect your ability to identify possible holding areas for largemouth in early spring. With a temperature gauge you will be able to locate the warmest bays on the lake. In early spring, this is often where you will find the most aggressive bass.

Temperature gauges can come as fancy as you wish. A digital read-out feature can take a lot more abuse than a needle-type display device. Even a simple hand held thermometer can be used to find the temperatures of water.

PH AND OXYGEN METERS

This is one group of gauges that is simply a waste of your money. Simply put, in our northern natural lakes, the same water conditions do not exist as in the reservoirs down south. To say that bass prefer one level of oxygen content in the water is not far fetched, but to go around the lake looking for an oxygen level that bass are supposed to like is a little off track. There are so many factors that can override the reading you receive, that it really doesn't pay to use it for the one chance in a hundred of it paying off. The same holds true for the acidic content of the water or "PH." If the water you are fishing is too acidic or too alkali, the fish will not be around. Unfortunately, you will never know what the PH level is where you are fishing because the levels can change at various depths with no way for you to know about the change until after you fish the area.

SCENT PRODUCTS

Over the last few years a lot of noise has been made by the makers of various lure scents. The products claim to have a fish-attracting smell. Having used all the products on the market today, I can say that I have never seen them make any difference in bass fishing. I know that many anglers will say, "How could he not believe?" The stories I have read are very convincing indeed, but I am the kind of guy who likes to find out for himself. In conducting my backyard tests, I have compared all of the major scent products. My study was done in my own pond where conditions are almost identical to those of a natural lake. Small sponges were soaked with the various scent products and spaced at three foot intervals with alternate sponges having nothing on them at all. I wanted to see if the bass were indeed attracted to the scent alone. After two weeks of testing under various conditions, I came to the same conclusion that I had in fishing. It didn't make any difference at all!

I have seen no adverse effect from adding these scent products, either. Although I try to keep gas and oil smells off my lures, with fish that demand live bait tactics, I feel that scent products can add more confidence to your fishing. Walleye fishermen note an increase in their success, and I have seen it happen when a product called "Fish Formula II" has been added to jigs.

One of the newest theories on scents for catching bass involves bass tasting the lure. The Mann's Bait Company has developed a product called FS-454. These folks feel that a bass is attracted to a lure by its action and not by the smell. Once a fish grabs the lure, it knows within a few seconds if it wants to eat the lure or not. FS-454 is a product that is supposed to make the bass want to eat the rubber worm it has been applied on. Their testing clearly shows that with other scent products, the bass will not hold or actually swallow the rubber worm for long. With their product, 100% of the time the bass would eat the worm!

This was very intriguing to me and I was very anxious to test this new material on the fish in my private pond. Within five minutes of testing I had three hits. Every time the bass held the worm for thirty seconds before I set the hooks! For a while, I thought that I had the unfair advantage. The bass were going crazy for this new taste product that was applied to my rubber worms. In all fairness to the study I stopped fishing the worm after catching three bass. I changed to a regular rubber worm that I had kept in a plastic bag for the last four years. Within five minutes I had taken another three bass, and each of them had also held the bait for at least thirty seconds before I set the hooks! My revolutionary breakthrough didn't last long, and I don't know what to say, other than that it sure seems like a good idea.

All and all, these scent products can give anglers a new confidence in their fishing. They can mask any fowl odors and add a new ray of hope on those slow days. Are scents the answer to our fishing dreams? Not quite, but they are fun to play with.

ODDS AND ENDS

Many of the little things that we don't give a thought to can greatly affect our success. Things such as having an anchor. Without an anchor in some situations, the odds of catching more than one fish from a spot would be nearly impossible. Take, for example, river fishing for smallmouth. The single best way to hold a boat out from a good eddy is to anchor. Anchors are a very important tool in boat control and definitely have a place in bass fishing.

A simple thing like a push-pole can make getting into and out of a tight situation a snap. Many of the larger, high performance boats draft a lot of water and can easily get blown into areas where they might get stuck. A push-pole has come to the rescue many a time and is a nice device to bring along.

Marker buoys give anglers a reference point that can make staying on a prime area possible. Bass fishing is often done along the shore, so shore markings can be used, but when you do some deep water bassin', it gets difficult to know exactly where you are.

Last, but not least, let us not forget any of the safety devices that everyone should have in their boat even if it is not required. Things such as life jackets, fire extinguishers, signal flares, horn, and lights for running at night. Bass fishing is a great sport, but it is not worth risking your life over.

CHAPTER EIGHT

SPECIALIZED BASSIN' TACTICS

This section of the book deals with many of the more commonly used methods and strategies for fishing bass. The North Country bass angler will face conditions much different than those found in the south. Although a bass is a bass, the way a bass reacts to northern conditions does call for some special tactics.

There are many variations to the methods we will discuss. Anglers with an open mind will be better able to modify these tactics to fit the situation at hand. It is my hope that each and every one of my readers will get a chance to try these methods in the season ahead.

Boat Dock Bass

Over the last five years, bass anglers in the north have become more aware of just how productive dock fishing for bass can be. This discovery of a prime shallow water bassin' hide-out has made for great fishing for those who know how to fish them.

There is no real bizarre reason for finding bass under boat docks. I know some people will come up with some big high power terms to explain why they do what they do, but it is really quite simple. Bass are creatures who like "things". This point has already been made. Anglers who are looking to find a good looking bass spot need to find areas which offer food, security, and comfort. To the underwater world of a bass, a boat dock is the perfect answer. Bass simply love boat docks, and the anglers who understand this love dock fishing.

When the big craze for dock fishing first hit the fishermen, experts were making bold statements about which docks the bass would like best. One would say that you need a wooden dock. Another would say that the dock had to be near deep water. This made dock fishing seem like you could predict which docks could hold bass. There are many factors which can increase the chances of the dock fisherman, but you can NEVER make hard rules.

Boat dock bass are home bodies that very seldom stray far from the protection and comfort of a shaded dock. Fishing during the middle of the day when the bass are grouped in the shade of the dock can be very productive. The key to success is making sure your casts are targeted as close to the dock posts as possible.

In my travels across the northland, boat dock fishing has been one of my most reliable places for finding bass. When you are heading out on a new lake, you should fish portions of the lake which look similar to places you have fished before, and a boat dock is often it. In docks, I can expect to catch both largemouth AND smallmouth, if they are present. I have learned that there are NO rules which can predict when a bass will be holding under a boat dock.

Some areas may have docks with only metal posts in knee-deep water that can hold a six pound largemouth. What should the fisherman do to find docks which are productive? The only answer is simply to fish all the docks! This may sound rather strange, but until you learn which areas are best for dock fishing, the only real way to find productive areas is to spend some time fishing each dock.

Obviously, some lakes are a little more productive for

dock fishing than others. I have found that bass tend to hang around boat docks more often when there isn't much cover along a shoreline. A good example of this is lakes which have beautiful sandy shores and lack a steep drop-off. The bass here like the shallow water and have no place else to find food, security, and comfort. In such lakes, you might not find bass in the shoreline docks as much as you will around the boat lifts or swimming platforms.

Anytime you find areas where it appears that there is no place else for the bass to hide, docks are the best areas to start fishing. Boat docks large and small can be productive.

A stretch of boat docks along a developed shoreline can often mean some great bassin'. Although you might get some strange looks from the residents, they will be shocked to see the bass that were living under their docks.

A dock is a perfect example of what I like to refer to as "visual structure". Fishing for bass in such areas is not so much a matter of selecting a secret lure, but rather a lure which can be fished effectively. The biggest single problem anglers face when fishing visual structure is the ability to cast accurately. The lures you use around boat docks could be spinnerbaits, rubber worms, or even shallow-running crankbaits.

The spinnerbait by far is the most popular lure around docks with its almost snagless nature and excellent castability. Rubber worms are great if you wish to fish slower around a favorite dock. Crankbaits work extremely well in areas where not too many weeds are around the dock posts which could foul the action.

Casting accuracy and boat positioning are the key factors in your fishing success with boat docks. More than once I have been forced to fish behind other anglers. This is when it pays to put lures a foot or two closer to the docks than the other anglers. There is no doubt that dock fishing will require practice before you will be able to catch bass on a regular basis.

Up until now, little has been said about boat control while fishing. With dock fishing, a very critical part of your success will depend on how the boat is positioned and maneuvered for maximum effect. You will need to compensate for wind and casting accuracy with each dock you approach. The skills you develop from dock fishing will also apply to fishing other forms of visual structure.

As you approach a boat dock the momentum of your boat should be stopped. Too many times the best casts are missed because anglers overshoot the dock and quite possibly spook the bass under the dock at the same time.

The most aggressive bass in a dock often sit on the outside edges of the dock facing outward. The first cast should be made not at the dock, but along the front face of the dock. Any time you fire a cast directly at something, you run a high risk of spooking the bass or just missing the target. Making casts at or under a dock takes a lot of practice, and I have personally found that it is just not worth it. By targeting your casts to run along the front face of the dock, you will expose your lure to the most aggressive fish. This may sound simple, but the fact of the matter is that your casts MUST be within inches of the dock posts as the lure is retrieved.

How the lure is retrieved is based on water depth and

Casting accuracy is very critical when aiming for a specific target. To be really effective at boat dock fishing or when you need to cast towards any object, the closer your lure can be, the better your chance for a strike.

many other factors which may effect the performance of the lure you use. Spinnerbaits are my favorite around docks. These lures can be fished fast for a while, and then be made to drop right in front of each dock post to trigger a strike.

    I am commonly asked how long I fish each dock. This is tough to answer with an exact number. Intuition is one of the things you will have to rely on the most. If the front face of the dock looks like it deserves two or more casts, make them. If for some reason you feel that your casts could have been a little closer, then make them a little closer. It usually takes two casts to cover the outside edge of the dock.

Casting your lures across the front face of a dock may sound simple, but there are many factors to consider before you make that first cast. Is your boat in a position so that you will be able to cast beyond the dock face? The longer the casts that you make, the less accurate you become. Make sure that you wait until the boat moves into a good position to make a cast behind the dock. Your ultimate goal is to retrieve the lure next to or hits each dock post.

In the back of your mind you must imagine a bass lying under the shaded dock. Any bass using the dock for a home has learned that there is never a need to stray into the sunlight to feed. Anything he could possibly need is **UNDER** the shade of the dock. Although bass will hang around docks during sunny and cloudy days, the bright sun tends to hold them tighter to the docks.

Knowing that a bass will not stray from the shaded portion of a dock, you must start planning your next cast. Casting your lures at the side of the dock is simply a waste of time! Even if you make a perfect cast to the base of a dock post, the lure is pulled out of the strike zone with the very first crank of the handle.

Again, it is to your advantage to target your casts so that they will run along the entire length of the dock. It is very important that the boat be positioned so you are able to cast straight down the dock. You may have problems stopping the boat's momentum as you move about, so your rod tip can be swung to the left or right to keep the lure running as close to the dock as possible. This simple act of swinging your rod tip from left to right can quickly make up for a cast that was slightly off target. Often one cast along the length

When casting along the length of the dock, be sure to use your rod tip to keep your bait running near the dock posts. By doing this you can often control the direction of your baits by five or six feet.

of a dock will be enough to see if there are any aggressive fish to be caught. As an extra bit of added insurance, you may want to make a cast to the other side of the dock.

Any bass that is at all aggressive will pounce on any lure that comes near it. In many ways, when you are dock fishing you are looking for only the aggressive bass. If, for some reason, you know a bass is holding under a dock, then slower tactics may be used. Rubber worms or jig & pig combos can often take the more finicky bass.

Docks with unique shapes often take more casts to cover properly. With a "T" dock, for example, you must cast the outside face and the inside corner of the "T" before you move the boat to a position to cast down the length of the dock.

Docks with big boat canopies are often prime ares for holding bass. In such areas the bass should be holding on the inside edges of the dock or under the boat itself. The use of spinning or spincast reels make casting under the canopies a lot easier with no fear of backlashes. I often crouch down on one knee so I am better able to fire a cast as far into the shaded area as possible.

Reaching a bass that is hiding under a canopy boat dock may mean dropping down onto one knee to cast. Getting your body into a better position to cast under a dock can mean the difference between catching or not catching a big bass. Good casting can be the biggest single factor in your bass fishing success around boat docks.

This brings me to explain the #1 cardinal rule in boat dock fishing. "First worry about hooking the bass, then worry about how you will get her out." Time and time again the use of twenty pound test line has been the only reason I have landed a bass which was hooked on the other side of a dock post or rope. Far too many people who fish docks worry about getting hung up, so they don't risk making the casts they should. With heavy line and a drag set as tight as it can go, the dock fisherman should be able to keep

When fishing around boat docks, it is very important that you really teach the bass who is in control. The bigger the bass, the more they will resist coming out from under a dock. That is why many anglers use twenty pound test line for dock fishing.

a steady pressure on the bass until he can go in to get it.

How far away should the boat be positioned from the dock while casting? This is a very good question, but the answer may vary for each fisherman. As I have explained, the longer the distance you cast, the less accurate you will be. My motto is to determine the distance I can reach with a "normal" cast. I position the boat so that the dock is about 1/3 the total distance of my casts. In clear lakes it pays to make longer casts to avoid spooking the bass. The easiest way to do this is to simply use a heavier lure rather than casting your arm off. In dirty water I have been within a few feet of the dock without spooking the bass underneath. One of my little tricks for fishing around docks with "L" or "T" shapes is to make my first cast along the front face and inside edge, but as I position the boat for the cast down the length, I put one foot on the dock so I am given time to complete my cast. If I do hook a fish I can quickly step out onto the dock and steer the fish around the posts.

When fishing an "L" shaped dock, one trick is to put a foot on the dock as you pass by. This is a practical way to keep you in a prime position to cast along the side of the dock. This, of course, is done after the front face of the dock has been fished.

Developing your own style of dock fishing also depends on the type of boat you are using. In all of the boat positioning talked about so far, electric motors mounted on the bow of the boat were used to move the boat around. Working into the wind, and not with it, is another little tip for better boat control. While making your casts allow for windage to keep your baits close to the dock.

Can more than one fish come from a dock? The answer is YES! The most I have ever taken was 21 fish! These bass were schooling under a small "L" shaped dock and I hooked a fish with 21 straight casts. I know this may sound a little strange, but to a dock bass, what goes on in the lake outside of their dock is of little importance. In many of the heavily traveled city lakes, the bass have grown accustomed to the sounds and noises of boat traffic. If a bass is taken quickly from under a dock and is not permitted to spook the others, it is possible to take one bass after another.

You can see how theories and rules can be blown right out of the water with just one fishing trip. I have learned my lesson when it comes to dock fishing. When I see a stretch of docks, I don't decide which docks are good and which are bad, I simply fish them all!

Bog Bass Fishing

Through much of the North Country, few lakes do not have some type of floating bogs or undercut weed edges. Many of the flowage lakes of northern Wisconsin are full of huge bogs which move about the lake as the wind blows.

These floating bogs and undercut banks offer some of the best areas to fish bass. On some lakes, it may be the ONLY place to catch bass. Anglers who learn how to fish bogs do well, anglers who do not will simply be skunked! A bog offers many of the same great qualities as a boat dock. Lots of food, security, and comfort. Bass may never see a need to leave the bog except for when they spawn.

One of the big problems is getting a lure to the bass that may be hiding under the blanket of weeds. We can fish the ones which are aggressive and near the outside edges. Many more will never see your lures no matter what technique is used.

A bog can be found floating over any depth of water. The only areas which should be of interest to the fisherman are the areas just under the bog. Many of the free floating bogs in northern Wisconsin have ten feet of water under them at all times. The bass relate not to the bottom, but to the under-side of the bog.

Since much more exact lure control is needed to present a lure to bog bass, the angler must position the boat very close to the bog edge. Casts should be made by slowly

Floating bog could be as small as some weeds blown along a shoreline after a wind to a major island of floating vegetation. The aggressive bass will take up position on the outside edges, but the large majority of bass will hold way under the blanket of weeds, making them impossible to fish. It pays to fish a bog shoreline several times a day to catch the bass that move to the outside edges to feed.

dropping lures along the bog edge. Several years ago I published a story in "Fins and Feathers" and later in the "In Fisherman", about applying a southern method of fishing called "flippin'" to our natural lakes. Flippin' can be easily brought into play when we are talking about bogs. Flippin' can be described as fishing so close to the area you want to fish that you simply flip the lure to the target. The boat is often not more than fifteen feet away as you swing the lure underhand to the edge of the bog. The lure is permitted to drop straight down until it reaches the bottom. At this point the lure is simply lifted out of the water and the procedure is repeated. You may be dipping your lure into a new spot every five seconds as you work along a bog edge.

Just as with dock fishing, casting at a bog is often very challenging but not very efficient. The key to any successful fishing method is to keep the lure in front of the fish for as long as possible. Casting at the bog will render the same poor results as with dock fishing. Casting along the length of the bog is a good idea, but the irregular shape of the bog makes casting difficult. The last resort to fishing productively is to use the flippin' method and position the boat close enough so that you will be able to drop the lure into the good looking pockets.

At this point, your boat maybe only five feet from the bog. Electric motors really are worth their weight in gold here. By moving along at a slow, steady pace, you lift the lure and drop it around every portion of the bog that you can reach. It is pure excitement when a five pound bass darts out from the bog to grab your lure. A jig & pig is the most popular lure choice when flippin' for bog bass. The slow dropping jig is heavy enough when out of the water to put where you want it, but when in the water it drops slow enough so that a bass can have time to see and attack it.

If two anglers are in the same boat, it is wise to have both anglers right in front so both will be able to stay close to the bog. Positioning the boat close to the bog scares far less fish than you might think. When using this flippin' method in the North Country, the longer the rod you have the better. Early bass anglers who fished bogs and heavy reed banks would use frogs on long cane poles. This a was called dabbling or dippin'. As you might imagine, flippin' is a big deal to tournament anglers, so manufacturers have designed rods that are 7 1/2 feet long for just this purpose. Tournament anglers would like to use longer rods, but there are restrictions on rod lengths in tournaments.

You need not own a specialized flippin' rod to fish bogs. Conventional spinning and bait casting outfits can work, but only for short periods. Anglers fishing bogs will find it to their advantage to use a longer rod for better lure and line control. After fishing only one small bog, you will

"Flippin'" for bass means getting in close to undercut banks and holding on when the big one hits. Anglers can get within a few feet of bass hiding under a bog and still get them to hit. A long rod with strong line is in order for this type of fishing.

recognize the advantages of longer rods. A bog bass will NEVER stray more than one foot from home to grab your lure. Remember that as you fish.

I must stress one last point for when you are out there working those bogs. BE CONFIDENT. Keep telling yourself that there is a bass in every pocket and you're going to catch it. Many may have a hard time believing you can be only a few feet away from a six pound largemouth and she will still strike. Don't sit in one spot for too long. Keep moving. Like with dock fishing, you are looking to catch the aggressive fish under a bog.

In my fishing I have taken only one smallmouth from under a bog. Smallmouth populations are often quite small in lakes which contain many boggy areas.

Fishing The Slop For Largemouth

The term often used in our natural lakes for describing very heavy weed cover is "slop". This term is used to describe any thick growth of weeds. In lakes where this ultra thick weed growth exists, anglers will find some very large bass. These super weedy areas form a summertime home for really big bass.

The weeds may seem to choke the surface, but if there are any open pockets, you can bet that there are some big bass holding down there. The secret to success in such areas is to make long casts and fish areas where you cannot see the bottom or the bass. If you can see the bass, the bass can see you and the odds of making them strike are greatly reduced.

Once spawning is complete, many bass start to group together in schools, while some prefer to remain loners. These loners are often the big females who like to take over a small area for the rest of the season and call it home. They move very little in or out of the weeds, being very content to feed on the large amount of panfish and minnows which also hide in the thick weeds.

Fishing super thick weeds for bass is a lot of fun, and with the right kind of equipment can be very productive. First, let's take a look at the boat. In such thick, shallow areas, it is wise to use a small, light boat that drafts little water. This will make it easier to maneuver in the thick weeds. In the kind of weeds I am talking about, there is no weedless electric motor that can run through it. In many cases, the only way to move about once you are inside the weeds themselves is with an oar or a push pole like those used by duck hunters. Ideally, you would like to find areas which you can reach by casting but still be able to use your electric motor for control. The wind is often the best aid in moving your boat through the weeds.

For rods and reels, the only choice is a stiff, preferably long casting rod with a bait casting reel. This will give you

A push-pole that is used by duck hunters can come in handy when you want to work those super thick weeds for bass. Although electric motors are fine in some weeds, often the only way to move your boat around in heavy cover is with a push-pole.

maximum casting distance. One of my favorite super-slop rods is a 7 1/2 foot Flippin' Stik. This is the same rod I described in the section on bog bass. This rod and reel combo, with at least twenty-pound test line, is perfect for fishing heavy weeds for bass.

For this style of fishing you will actually need two different outfits if you fish by yourself. One will be rigged with a super weedless bait like the Moss Boss, and the other will be rigged with a weedless topwater bait like a Super Frog.

Your goal is a simple one: to cast that Moss Boss as far as you can into the weeds with the big rod. You want to simply drag this bait across the tops of the weeds. The pace should be brisk as you skitter the lure across the surface. In the maze of weeds below, there could be a bass almost anywhere. Predicting where a bass will be is impossible. To find out where the bass are hiding, you will need to cover as much of the weedy surface as you can.

Moving your boat to a central location, start systematically casting from one side to the other, spacing your casts about ten feet apart. You will be looking for any signs of fish activity at all. It could be a swirl near your lure as it skips along, or a wake behind the bait.

Simply put, you are looking to find a bass. Many times you will get the bass to grab at your Moss Boss but miss it. It is not the fault of the lure or the fisherman. In such heavy cover, it becomes hard for the bass to get a good bead on his target. A bass will keep after the bait if he is mad enough.

If you do see a boil or other sign of bass activity, quickly grab your rubber frog and throw it as close to the disturbance as possible. I will often use a weedless rubber worm for the same purpose. Once a bass is located in heavy cover, there is a very good chance it will strike the second offering.

After a hard day of slop fishing, expect your arms to be a

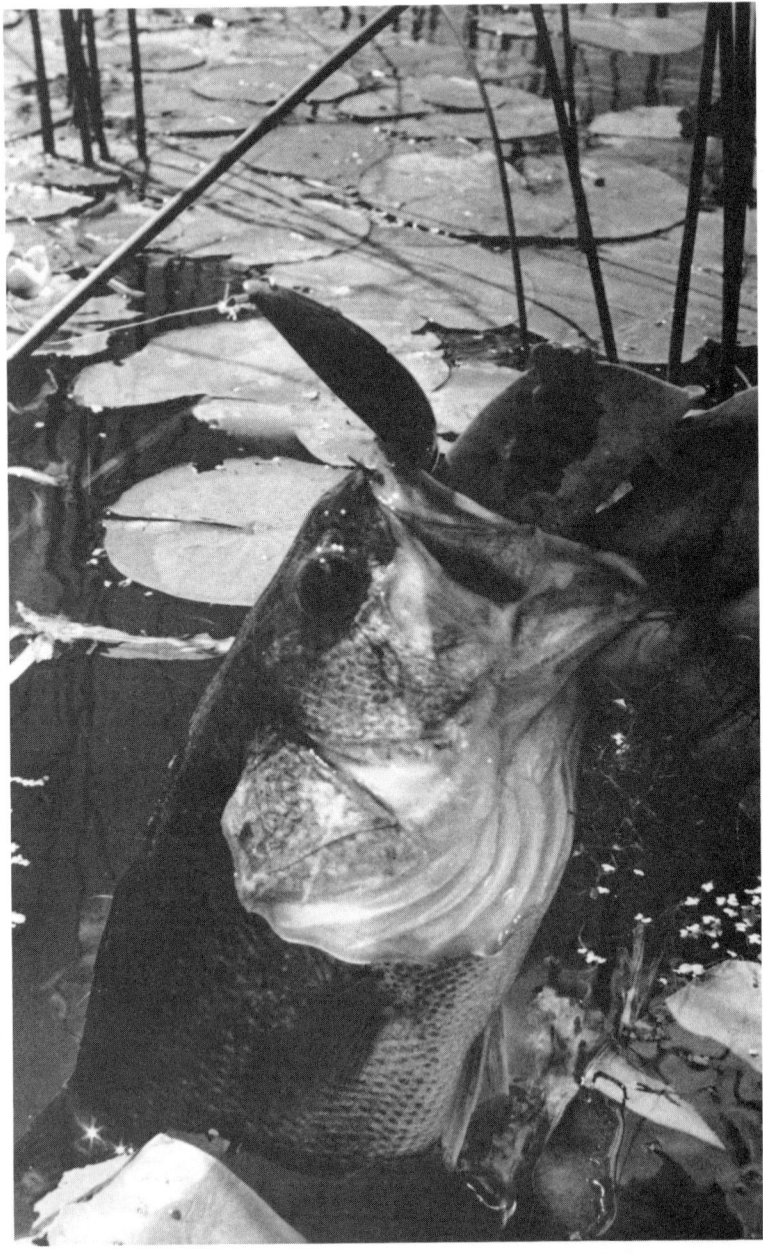

In super thick weeds, a Moss Boss is a top choice. When fishing such heavy cover, heavy line and a tight drag is critical to landing even a small bass.

little sore. The secret to success is making those super long casts. After a few hours of casting, it can seem a lot like work. Never take your eyes off the lure as it travels across the surface. Some of the biggest bass you will take often make the smallest ripples.

Bass in Reeds

One of the advantages in fishing natural lakes is the wide variety of weeds you will encounter. Many people may hate fishing weeds, but a bass fisherman MUST learn to live with them. In many of the cleaner lakes, the shallows are full of reeds. There is a difference between reeds and bulrushes. The easiest way to tell the difference is by looking at the stalks. The stalk of a reed is round whereas the stalk of bulrush is flat like a blade of grass. Reeds prefer to grow from hard bottomed areas and rushes, are found in mucky or soft bottomed areas. Most bogs consist of rushes not reeds.

Note the difference between the reeds on the left and the rushes on the right. Reeds have round stalks and grow from sandy or even gravel bottom areas. Rushes look like giant stalks of grass and prefer to grow in muddy bottomed areas or in bogs.

The reed is quite fragile in that if water conditions are not right, they will die off. They form one of the most common hideouts for North Country bass. Catching bass from a patch of reeds is not too difficult at all, as long as you know what to look for.

Electric trolling motors will make your task of covering water very simple. The equipment best suited for this type of fishing is heavy bait casting gear. The reeds are tough and a big bass knows that when hooked, the only way to escape is to hide in the weeds. If, by chance, you do not fish with a tight drag and the bass is permitted to run, the bass

Dusk is one of the prime times for fishing reeds. The bass simply love to cruise the outside edges of the reeds looking for an easy meal. The memories of fishing at times like this is what makes our long winters bearable.

could get free. It is extremely important to remember this when fishing reeds or any heavy cover for that matter. Anytime you fight a bass where they must be brought through or over some heavy cover, you MUST keep the fish on top and its head above the water. If the bass is permitted to turn downwards, the chances of him getting off greatly increase.

This method of shuffling a big bass in is often referred to as the "Zenanko shuffle" by my friends. By reeling fast, you are able to keep a big bass moving right through heavy cover without snagging up.

In reed fishing, you can use several different lures with fairly good success. Looking at each situation as it arises is the best way to decide which lure combination is right for you. In areas where the reeds are in very shallow water, a topwater lure might be an excellent choice. In areas where the reeds are spread out over a large area, a spinnerbait would cover more water than any other lure. In areas where the reeds run deep and seem to form a wall, a rubber worm would be a great choice to fish along the base of the reed stalks.

Fishing a tangled mass of reeds can be a little frustrating. More times than not it is best to concentrate your efforts on the outside edges of the weed growth. It seems that bass pack up more on the outside than on the inside. When bass move from one area of the reeds to another, they travel the outside edge. The occasional lone bass will be found deep inside the reeds, but the largest groups will be on the edges. Bass anglers rigged with different lures will be able to adjust to the changes in reed growth as they occur.

The "prime" areas are always irregular shapes or clumps of thick weed growth. Anglers should always be on the lookout for these areas while they cast along a shoreline. As with fishing boat docks and bogs, you must fire your casts beyond the reed pocket you wish to fish and bring the bait back through the area as close to the reed

Stalks of reeds can make the ideal home for bass. Although the reeds could form a large tangled mass to hide bass, the majority of the catchable fish will hold close to the outside edges. As with all shallow water cover, the bass will prefer to wait in ambush points like a small point or pocket in the reed bank. Your casts should be directed to these areas for best success.

stalks as possible.

Feel free to play some games with the way you retrieve the lures. Pause, and let the baits drop, or buzz them along the surface. In many cases it will be impossible to cast along the edges of the reeds like you can with boat docks. This is the one occasion where you might be forced to cast directly at a wall of reeds. As you might imagine, if a strike occurs it will happen within one foot of the reed stalks. These reed bass are more prone to chase a bait that is running away from the reeds, but don't let this be an excuse for not fishing close.

It is quite common to see several bass follow a hooked bass out from the reeds. These other bass can be easily caught if your partner sees them soon enough. The other bass think that the hooked fish is simply running away from the school and doesn't wish to share. It is a great sign to see a school of bass chasing a hooked fish. Although you may spook the other fish away, after a short period of time those bass will be back in the same area feeding again.

Since you may be forced to fish reed areas by casting directly at the reeds, a quick-fire method of fishing is a great trick. Rubber worm fishermen often use this method because it makes worm fishing into a surprisingly fast way to cover water. As the boat moves long the edge of the reeds, the angler fires a cast to the base of the reed stalks. The worm is permitted to reach the bottom, and if nothing strikes the lure, it is quickly retrieved. This procedure is repeated over and over at any likely looking notch or point in the reed bank. Since the bass will very seldom travel more than a foot away from the reeds to grab your bait, there is no need to waste a lot of time fishing the bait all the way to the boat.

When fishing a bank of reeds, it is critical keep your drag set tight to bring the bass towards you as soon as possible. Remember, a high percentage of the strikes you will receive come from within one foot of the reeds. It may pay not to spend a great deal of time fishing a lure once it gets about three feet out from the reed stalks.

Although is takes a little practice to get your speed and accuracy up to par, it is a very effective way to fish. Open face spinning tackle is very popular for this purpose, especially in deeper reeds. A big problem when you use bait casting gear for casting to such targets is that the lure reaches the water with a tight line. As the lure sinks, the tightness in the line will cause the lure to swing away from the base of the reeds. If the bass are riding high you may not notice a problem, but if they are holding tight, it may be hard to get the lure in front of a bass. With spinning tackle there is always a certain amount of slack in your line to permit the lure you use to drop straight down.

There is no rule written that says the bass need to always be on the outside edges of the reeds. Many of the most avid bass anglers prefer to fish the inside edges for their bass. Like with boat dock fishing, it is not wise to write off an area until you have had a chance to fish all of it first. What looks like water void of bass may actually hold the biggest bass in the lake!

RIVER SMALLMOUTH TACTICS

The power of a fighting smallmouth bass is never stronger than of those taken from a river. Skilled at using the current to their every advantage, the smallmouth becomes a very challenging fish to land. Many anglers would rather fish rivers than any other type of water. Rivers hold a special kind of romance and challenge for the fisherman. Any angler who can master river fishing techniques can be deadly on lakes, but not necessarily the other way around. Anglers will need to develop a special style of boat control and a keen awareness for lure control as well.

Many of our North Country smallmouth streams are very accessible by simply walking the banks. One of the best ways to fish some of the shallow water streams with a boat is to stop from time to time to walk the bank. Having been raised on the banks of the Mississippi River, I was bitten by an addiction to river fishing at a very young age. Even as an adult, the most enjoyable times I have fishing are on rivers.

Smallmouth love to feed near the edge of boiling whitewaters. Anglers are advised to bring the baits as close to the bottom as possible with the current to present the baits as naturally as possible. A river flowing into a lake is one of the more consistent smallmouth spots. Smallmouth just love to feed near current. Knowing this can make finding smallmouth very easy to locate on some lakes.

Because of a lifetime spent river fishing, I find it hard to describe all my tricks in just one small section of this book. What I will try to do is to hit on the most important factors which control your success, and then you'll be able to develop your own style from there.

Boat Control In Current

Water levels control smallmouth location on rivers. The higher the water is, the tighter they will hold to obstructions in the river current. River smallmouth will seldom stray far from moving water. Even during low water times when current levels are not that strong, smallmouth will move out to areas next to the current.

Boat control is, of course, an important factor in catching bass. The better the position you are in to make a cast behind current breaks, the more your odds increase. Fishing current obstructions at long range is very difficult indeed. The water flow will grab your line and lure and swing them out of position. Fishing close to your target is very important in river fishing.

One of the simplest, but yet effective, ways to fish a river is to drop anchor. By positioning your boat either parallel to or just downstream from the area you wish to fish is the best way to cover an area. Over the past few years veteran river angler Dan Gapen has been promoting the use of motors for boat control. His method is called "slipping". All you do is back the boat into the flow of the current and increase the speed of the motor until the boat hovers in one spot. This method does take a little practice in order to fish and control the boat at the same time.

On my river boat I have a ten foot length of rope and a ten pound "U" shaped anchor. Very seldom will I be fishing waters deeper than four or five feet when fishing river smallmouth. When I approach an area such as a big boulder or eddie current behind a point, I simply motor slightly upstream from the current break and drop the

A limit of smallmouth can come easily if good boat control is used to hold you in the proper position. Far too many people tend to drop anchor and fish anywhere, and that can mean a lot of fishless days.

anchor. The boat floats back until the anchor grabs.

The boat used is also critical to your ease of positioning. A canoe is very easy to work in shallow water, but is tough to fish from. Regular "V" bottomed fishing boats often draft too much water for the shallow portions of the river, and the "V" shaped hull will permit the current to grab the boat and spin it around when you least expect it. The smaller fishing boats up to 14 feet can work very nicely in most rivers that are not too shallow. Boats made of fiberglass will be quickly scratched by the rocks, and they also draft a lot of water which makes these boats almost impossible to use in shallow rivers. By far the #1 choice for river fishing is the family of Jon boats. These flat bottomed aluminum boats draft little water, are stable to fish from, and are excellent to handle in current.

With river boats, speed is not a critical factor. In many cases it is best to move from place to place slowly to prevent damage to the boat and the lower unit of the motor. Many anglers have installed special prop protectors when fishing a rocky smallmouth stream. These metal bars or doughnuts, which are attached to the lower units act as a kick up device to prevent the motor from smashing directly into a rock.

Lures and Their Presentations On River Smallmouth

For proper lure and line control, you will never want to cast downstream to your target. It is always best to cast either upstream or cross-stream for best success. This will not only make lures like the crankbaits run better, but will present the lures in a more natural fashion with the current.

As you work lures through and along the edges in the current keep a steady pressure on your line. Anytime you cast upstream the lure is free to drop to the bottom and be snagged. This is by far the toughest part of river fishing. Learning to control the drop and action of your lures to prevent snagging is very difficult.

Jig fishing with rubber grubs is very effective on river smallmouth. Many of the prime waters where the old bronzebacks hang out are also full of jig eating rocks and logs. To make it easier to fish in such areas the angler can do three things to prevent getting snagged as often.

1. Use a lighter weight jig. Lighter jigs are harder to cast, but will permit a slower drop and less snags.

2. Use heavier line. The larger the line diameter, the more water resistance it has to slow the drop of your jigs.

3. Add a spinner. This little tip actually changes the action of the bait, but it is very effective. The kind of spinner I am talking about is like those found on a beetle spin type of lure(see photo). The spinner acts like a parachute and also slows the drop of your jig to the bottom.

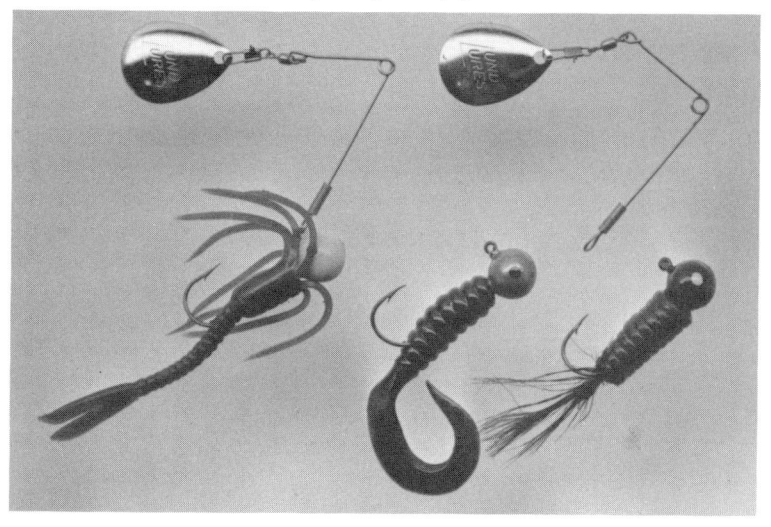

A beetle-spin type of bait can be made by adding a spinner to any type of grub bodied jig. This little trick makes it possible to fish a jig over the tops of rocks and snags. Smallmouth really have a hard time refusing a jig and spinner combination.

In river fishing, there are often just three groups of lures to choose from: Jigs, spinners, and crankbaits. When you are jig fishing it is best to bring along several dozen 1/8 and 1/4 ounce jigs. In the spinner family, the Beetle Spin is simply deadly on river smallmouth. The best sizes are 1/16 to 1/4 ounce, depending on the action of the rod you are using. The family of in-line spinners such as the Mepps and Panther Martin spinners, are also very effective. Within the crankbait group, it is often best to stay away from deep divers. The current can really mess up the action of a deep diving crankbait. It is best to stay with the shallow runners, especially those with a very tight wiggling action. The Cordell Spot is one of my favorites for fishing rivers, as is the shallow running Wee-R from Rebel.

Crayfish patterned lures are always a good bet on smallmouth. White rubber grubs are also a personal favorite on my jigs. But you can never go too far wrong by using lure colors that match the favorite foods of bass.

As you travel from spot to spot, always be aware of boating hazards. Watch for rocks and logs, especially when there is wave action on the surface to reduce your ability to spot these obstructions. Learning to read the water is all part of learning to river fish. Just by looking at a stretch of river, you should be able to identify the deepest route to travel and the best areas to fish within a quarter mile. The countless variety of places a smallmouth can hide is what

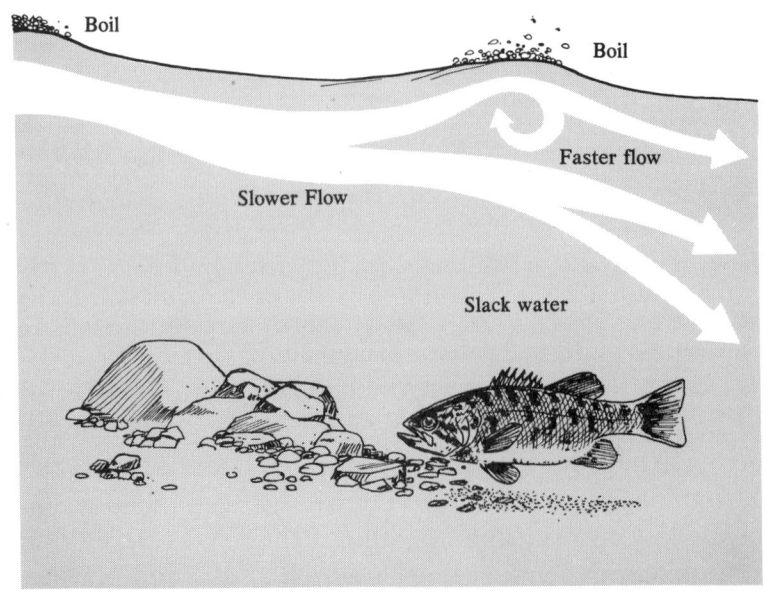

Any type of current break can hold a smallmouth. The key to success is understanding where the slack water actually is that the fish are holding behind. Smallmouth are just waiting to grab your baits if they are presented with the current in a natural manner.

makes river fishing so exciting. Just when you think you have fished the best spot on the river, you come around a bend and find six spots that look even better!

Late summer is by far the most prime time to be on the river after smallmouth. Water levels are often at a very low point, eliminating many areas a river bass might hide out. Time and time, again the use of polarized sunglasses becomes priceless. You will often be able to spot fish holding in obstructions. These glare-reducing glasses makes it easier to fish "visible structure", but they do much more. In low water conditions it is possible to actually spot the bottom and know how deep the water is you are fishing or casting to. This kind of awareness will help prevent lure snagging and permit better line and lure control in current.

Most river fishermen do not need or use any electronic depth finding devices. These river rats rely on their ability to read the water and use only their fishing rods to determine river depth. Watching an avid river fisherman work an area, you will notice that from time to time he will insert the rod into the water to see if he can touch bottom. To many river fishermen, this is the way of check river depths.

In late September and early October, the smallmouth in our northern area start grouping in the deeper holes of the river. I have found the use of an electronic depth finder extremely valuable at this time of year. You can almost bet that every smallmouth within a half mile of a deep hole will be schooling in or near it as the leaves fall from our trees. Although the action may last for only two or three weeks at best, this can be some of the best fishing of the year.

Big Rivers for Smallmouth

Many of the larger rivers hold fantastic numbers of smallmouth. The key to success in this type of fishing water is to break the big river into smaller pieces. Many of the larger and wider stretches of river are maintained by the Army Corp of Engineering. These navigational channels prevent sand bars from building up that could make barge travel impossible.

There are many different man-made current deflectors which Corp uses to keep the river flowing in the right direction. Some, called "wing dams", are rock ridges extending out from shore. Wing dams come in many different sizes and shapes. Before fishing any river that has a maintained boat channel, be sure to check a river map to learn the shape of each dam.

Fishing a wing dam is really no different than fishing a pile of rocks on a shallow stream. The only difference is that you will need to reposition the boat several times in order to fish the entire eddy current. One of the big advantages to fishing big river smallmouth is that once you find one fish, you can find several more in the same eddy current. The large rivers often have very unique forms of current breaks. Always keep an open mind when you head out onto a big river. Stay alert for mooring posts, roots of a

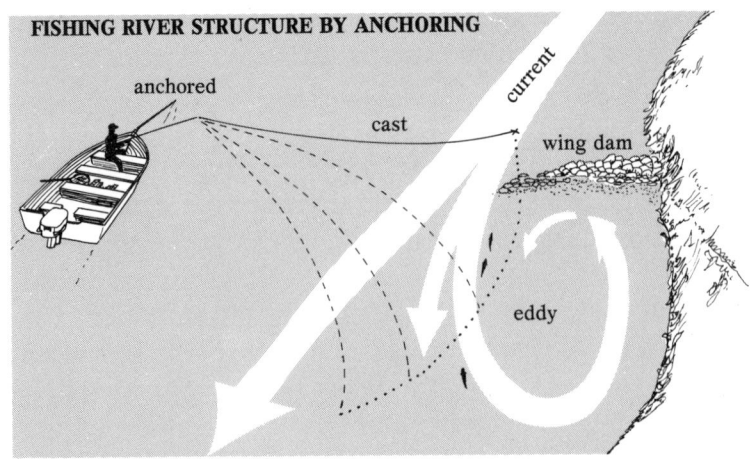

FISHING RIVER STRUCTURE BY ANCHORING

Using an anchor to hold a boat in current is a very practical way to fish obstructions in a river. This diagram shows just one position to hold in to fish a wing dam found on many larger rivers. It often is a good idea to re-anchor several times to reach all parts of a large current break.

fallen tree, or maybe even a storm sewer pipe. All of these types of areas can be hot spots for smallmouth.

One of the other prime smallmouth waters on a river is a shoreline of "rip-rap". Usually rip-rap is made from medium size rock. In some cases cracked cement blocks are used. These are placed in areas that receive a lot of current and the bank might normally wash away.

The steep banks of a rip-rap shoreline can hold a very large number of smallmouth. The vast majority of the smallmouth come from waters of five feet or less, even though the channel may drop off to 25 feet.

Since smallmouth could be hiding anywhere along a shoreline of rocks, it is often best to keep moving and target your casts to reach very close to shore. Ideally, you will want to cast straight upstream so that your lure runs tight along the rip-rap for the entire cast. Like in dock fishing, the longer your lure is in the most productive water, the better your chances are of getting a strike.

Often electric trolling motors are not strong enough to hold a boat in the main current of the river. If this is the case, use a gas motor while using the "slipping" method of boat control. The use of anchors in shallow water is a very good idea, but in twenty feet of water it gets to be hard work.

In rivers big and small, the style of fishing you use is very similar. For best results position your boat so that your casts are upstream or cross-stream. As you fish, try to always stay in contact with the bottom. Time and time again you will be snagged, but don't get discouraged. The more you learn about line and lure control, the less often the rocks will get away with your lures. Visual structure is visual structure no matter what kind of water you are on. By staying aware of any obstructions in the current, you will be better able to find smallmouth.

Trolling for smallmouth can be done in many of the shallower rivers. In such situations, it is possible to take bass from current breaks located tight to the bottom in midstream. Casting to these areas is often not very productive. This is due to the fact that over half your casting time may be spent on just getting the bait to the bottom. Trolling increases the time the lure spends on the bottom, and in turn increases the odds of catching a bass.

In a moving water situation it is rare indeed to take a bass from waters deeper than ten feet. It is common to be trolling only twenty feet behind the boat in five feet of water and be catching smallmouth. It seems that in rivers, a smallmouth feels very secure while hiding behind a rock. Your boat could be right above the bass and they will still dart out to strike a lure. This shows just how important it is that your lures be close to the bottom at all times.

This may seem rather contrary to what I have been stressing about having the lures traveling **WITH** the current to seem more natural. In trolling, it is best to troll **UPSTREAM!** By working slowly upstream in a zig-zag pattern, you are able to present the bait to more bass than by trolling straight upstream. Watch the shoreline, this will be your only way of judging boat speed. River currents can easily play tricks on you and make you think you are moving at great speeds, when actually you are standing still.

The goal of any good river troller is to work from side to side on the river at a crawling pace. Since the bait is coming from behind the bass, who always look upstream, it is critical to troll slowly. This will give the bass time to see and react to the bait. Crankbaits, which are the #1 choice for trolling, will be working like crazy in the current. At no other time will the tuning of crankbaits be more important. Some of your crankbaits will simply not run well against a current. Often the crankbaits which do the best job are those with a very tight wiggling action.

When you are fishing around rocks, it is very important to check your line for nicks and abrasions almost constantly. River bottoms with all their pesty snags, will cost you several of your favorite lures no matter what you do. Anytime you notice a nick in the line, cut your lure off and retie. By using a tough abrasion-resistant line such as Stren, you will loose fewer lures and fish.

CHAPTER NINE

WEATHER AFFECTS ON BASS

Bad weather on the horizon can often mean some great fishing for summertime bass anglers. Be aware that a sudden thunderstorm can be very dangerous. Bass are definitely affected by weather, and knowing how to adjust your tactics to match the weather will mean better success for the fisherman.

Day to day weather changes can greatly affect the locations of bass. This, of course, also plays a major role in the bass anglers' success. We have already reviewed what goes on over the course of a year for seasonal changes, but not daily weather conditions.

Wind, sun and rain all affect bass in different ways, and to some extent, how they react is controlled by seasons. One good example of this is bass activity in the fall. The best time to be out bass fishing is when the weather is the worst! Those beautiful Indian Summer days are nice to be outside but are poor for catching bass. Rain, wind, and even snow seem to excite the bass into feeding late in the season.

Lets first take a look at wind and how it affects your bass

fishing success. Wave action on lakes with rock points or shorelines is an ideal situation. Many times these areas of shallow rocks will only hold groups of bass when there is a brisk wind blowing over them. Wave action in vegetation such as reeds and rushes is not good at all. The constant swaying of the weeds makes the bass nervous. Although they might still be holding outside such areas when two and three foot waves are rolling through, you are often best advised to fish the calm side of the lake if the same type of vegetation exists.

One of my secrets for catching bass along a wind blown shoreline is to fish stationary objects. A boat dock piling or a bridge post is often used by the bass on windy days. They actually seem to move out of the rolling weed beds to seek out such areas.

Smallmouth, especially, seem to be stimulated by wave action. The pounding waves force their favorite food, the crayfish, out from under the rocks so they can gobble them up. The only trick to fishing a wind blown shoreline for bass is to realize that the bass could easily be in only one foot of water! I have taken four pound smallies from rocks that appeared to be in only six inches of water! The bigger the rocks, the better for attracting bass when there is a wind.

To the anglers who fish the bays, the wind is often a nuisance. To the anglers fishing the points, the wind is an advantage that many anglers look for. Every lake will be affected differently by wind, and wind can influence where the bass will school as well. Even though fishing becomes more challenging as you fight a twenty mile-per-hour wind, more times than not, good wave action is more an advantage than a disadvantage.

For years a rainy day has been looked upon as a good time to be on the water. Having spent many hours outdoors in the rain, I must agree that bass fishing can be very good then. Shallow water bass are more readily taken because they are less aware of your presence. The drops of rain reduce their visibility and confuse the sounds that bass may take as a warning. During a rain storm, bass seem to ride very high in the weeds, which makes it easier to get a bait to them. I have not seen much of a difference in bass activity while fishing a wind blown shoreline when it is raining, or when it is not. The rolling waves tend to break up water visibility enough so that rain isn't a major factor. Rain can especially work to your advantage on a calm day. You will be able to fish bass around shallow cover and find them in a very catchable mood.

Being out on the water when thunderstorms are coming is just plain foolish. A bass is NEVER worth risking your life for, and no matter how much you may want to stay on the water, GET OFF!

Cold Front Tactics

By far the most severe weather condition a bass angler could face is called the "cold front". The effects of a cold front are most noticeable during the summer when air and water temperatures are the warmest. After several days of warm, sunny weather, bass get into a routine of feeding. As a storm approaches, they seem to work themselves into a feeding frenzy. Anglers who fish just before storms move in often have some great action. When the bass are "on" like this, you wish the action would never end, but the next day the bass seem to have disappeared. The storm that came through during the night changed all that. After the storm left, the air temperature dropped twenty degrees, and the sky is now bright blue. These are the signs of a cold front, and the signs that anglers are not too anxious to experience during their annual vacation.

The drop in temperature, coupled with the super bright sun, have turned the bass off like a switch. Anglers who go out on the water should follow these steps if they hope to find a bass:

1. Fish lighter and smaller lures (live bait is a good bet now).
2. Use lighter lines.
3. Fish closer to any objects that bass may hang around.
4. Fish slower, don't hurry to cover a lot of water.
5. Work hard, a good day may mean only a few fish now.

When the water temperature is cooler, the affects cold fronts have on bass are lessened, such as the spring and fall when we may have a near freezing night, but the air will warm to the sixties by noon.

Water clarity also seems to play a factor in how a lake responds to a summer cold front. The dirtier the water, the less the bass are affected by cold fronts as they pass through. Many bass anglers prefer to fish stained waters in general for bass just because the action is more consistent.

It is hard to put a finger on which factors are the ones which can affect your bass fishing success the most. Is it the super bright sun, the drop in temperature, or the storm itself that shut off the action? There is one theory that stems from water temperature and insect activity that makes a lot of sense. The insects in any lake form the foundation of food for the minnows and baitfish that bass feed on. A drop in water temperature can shut down the insect hatches and scatter the baitfish. The bass seem to know that the food supply will be slim after the storm, so they feed like crazy. As the cold front passes, the minnows and baitfish scatter, making it hard for the bass to find food, so they simply rest until things become more stable.

Air temperature is not the deciding factor when judging whether a lake has recovered from a cold front or not. It is the stable and consistent weather. Once we have had three days of almost identical weather, the bass will have adjusted and will be back into a feeding routine.

Cold fronts have little affect on moving water. I recognized this long before I read about it in a book. River fishing after a storm may be a little tough if a lot of rain came with the storm because a lot of debris will be floating down the river. The smallmouth, especially, don't change their location if a storm swells a river for a day or so. The trick to catching them is to fish closer and tighter to the areas where they were holding before the storm hit. The use of a heavier jig or deeper diving crankbaits will get this done nicely. You will be surprised to see just how aggressive they can be.

No matter what the day is like, you should still try to wet a line. Fishing is ment to be a learning experience. No person can predict bass movements without actually going out onto the water to fish.

CHAPTER TEN

TOURNAMENT FISHING STRATEGIES

In the southern regions of the United States, bass fishing tournaments are big business. Thousands of dollars are on the line each week for the angler who can come to the weigh-in with the heaviest bag of bass.

Tournament fishing in the North Country has seen many different phases. Experts predict that because there is a lack of large lakes in the northern states we will never be big in bass tournaments. Although the northern regions of the country may not attract the big money contests, there are still many well run regional tournaments that can offer up to $3,000 for first place.

It is my firm belief that tournament fishing is good for the sport and great for your personal development as an angler. There is no better way to test your skills at bass fishing. Anglers who fancy themselves as sharp anglers love tournament fishing because they can pick up little tips to increase their own success in future tournaments.

The bass is a very valuable resource that should never be wasted, and for this the bass tournaments are perfect. The bass is one fish which can take the rigors of being caught, kept in live wells, and then released safely after being weighed. Bass organizations all over the north and south stress the importance of releasing every fish that is caught. Records show that easily 90% or more of all the fish taken during a bass tournament are released to fight again.

The true tournament fisherman is not at all interested in fishing for the meat, but for the challenge and sport of catching a bass. Live bait is strictly forbidden in tournaments because artificials are a better test of their skills, and at the same time, increase the chances of the bass being

Catch and release fishing with largemouth and smallmouth bass is made even easier because the bass can be handled by inserting your thumb in the mouth of the bass and grabbing the lower jaw. The bass can then be easily handled to remove the hooks, and the bass can be released back into the lake.

released healthy. With live bait, bass often get hooked too deeply and can die if the hooks are not removed properly.

Rules for each bass tournament may vary slightly, but many of the better run tournaments follow the B.A.S.S. (Bass Anglers Sportsman Society) tournament rules. These rules govern every possible problem that may occur during the tournament. Basically, anglers are paired together at random to fish. They are required to be courteous and follow a long series of safety rules to insure a safe and fair contest. The bass are kept alive in live wells if they meet the minimum length standards set by the tournament committee. Here in the North Country, the bass must exceed 12 inches in length. They are measured by keeping the mouth of the bass closed and if any portion of the tail exceeds 12 inches, it is a keeper. At the end of the day, the angler with the heaviest stringer of bass wins!

Tournament anglers need to carry a measuring device of some type with them during competition to make sure the bass meet the minimum size to become keepers.

Penalties vary for each tournament if you are late or if you have violated one of the rules. It pays to study the contest rules completely, because it could cost you first place if you are only one minute late!

Bass fishing tournaments are safe, fun, and exciting for those who compete and as mentioned earlier, you can really become a great bass fisherman in a shorter period of time.

Competing in a tournament and actually winning is something first time anglers dream about, but the true fact of the matter is, you should expect the first two years of tournament fishing to be "break in" years where you learn to handle the pressures of finding and catching bass on a consistent basis. You might be a great bass fisherman right now, but that does not mean you will be a great tournament bass fisherman. Fishing for sport and for money are two different things, so it takes a few years to develop a new way of thinking.

The weigh-in at a tournament often attracts a big crowd. Once the day of tournament fishing is over, the weights for each team or individual are listed on the score board. This is the scene for a lot of fish stories about "the one that got away".

Team or Individual Competition

More and more, tournaments in the north are becoming team fishing events with two anglers fishing in each boat. Although many of the avid tournament anglers would rather see individual competition where you draw for partners, team competition seems to be the wave of the future and seems to be the only way most tournaments can draw a large number of entries in the north. Many anglers prefer not to share their favorite hot spot with a stranger or be stuck fishing out of a strange boat.

The strategies you will use to be successful may also depend on the tournament being a one or two day affair. If you are starting to get the idea that tournament fishing strategies are complicated, you're RIGHT! There are countless factors which will directly affect your success in a tournament situation. This intrigue keeps some fishermen hard-core tournament anglers, traveling from one tournament to another all summer long. To the readers of this book who someday hope to be a major tournament contender, I must stress the importance of practice. As in many things in life, to really be good at something, you must take the time to work at it. Luck is something that is not given to you, YOU must work for it. To be a true contender, you must develop your skills to include all aspects of bass fishing known today. If, for example, you're fishing a lake that is full of reeds, you must be able to fish a spinnerbait. You must also learn to fish a rubber worm in the same situation. Some lakes are great for crankbaiting, so you must develop your skills with crankbait fishing until you feel you could catch a fish on every cast. All of the styles and methods of fishing artificial lures in this book should be mastered if you ever hope to successfully fish money tournaments.

I can cite many examples of very good anglers who place very high in tournaments when the bass can be caught with spinnerbaits. But when worm fishing is producing all the fish, these anglers might as well call it a day. No matter how many times I write it, the importance of VERSATILITY should never be taken lightly. Being a versatile angler simply means you will be able to adjust to the daily changes in fish activity to become a more consistent angler. It is nice to win a tournament, but if you can consistently place in the top ten in fishing competition, you are truly a skilled angler and it will only be a matter of time before you take first place.

In getting yourself ready to fish a tournament, I have found that there are four major rules to follow to aid in making yourself into a successful tournament fisherman.

1. Pre-fish waters
2. Do your own thing
3. Develop a game plan
4. Hard work

Fishing tournaments in the upper midwest often take place on only a handful of different lakes. In many cases you may have already fished the tournament waters before and think you have a good idea of where to fish. One of the mind games you must deal with when the time nears for the tournament involves approaching the lake as if you have never fished it before.

This is a common reason anglers who are "local experts" bomb out in a tournament situation. Every tournament must be fished in such a way that you start from scratch every time so you will not overlook the obvious. In most tournaments, contestants are not permitted to fish the area until three days before the competition. Many weekend warriors complain about this rule because they are often not permitted enough time to pre-fish the lake. The three days just before the contest begins will give you enough time to zero in on the most effective ways of fishing for the one or two days of competition ahead.

In fishing the same lakes year after year in competition, it is easy to use one method or fish only one area year after year because you have confidence in it. I must again stress the importance of starting from scratch each time you approach tournament fishing.

Lake maps are generally your best way of taking an objective look at the area and analyze where the fish might be. Past experience on the lake should guide you to the first areas you check out to determine if any fish still remain in the same areas. At no time should you EVER go back to these areas again while pre-fishing! Far too many areas are beat to death by anglers just checking an area to see if fish are there. I have fished with several anglers who would fish their best spots two or three times a day taking three or more keeper size fish each time, and get upset when Saturday rolls around and a fish can't be found.

If you are familiar with an area and feel it has some potential, don't beat it to death! It is very important that while pre-fishing you do not make it your daily goal to catch a limit of fish. Your goal is simply to find the fish, leaving the catching to the day of the contest.

The pre-fish period will enable you to explore areas around your hot spot or learn the exact shape of a bar or reef. During competition you will need to know exactly where everything is located at all times. This is especially true in individual competition where you may be fishing against a very good fisherman in your own boat. Memorize the weed beds and turns in the bottom contour by using land markers or your depth finder. When you are in charge of the boat, you must be aware of all prime areas before your partner finds them and takes one of your fish. You can bet he will be doing the same to you when his time comes to run the boat. Don't let your partner's "good old boy" outward appearance mislead you, because he wants more than anything to out fish YOU, too!

Learning and knowing a lake in every detail is great, but don't chase past catches around. It is easy to keep saying, "I know they're here, I just have to make them bite". Many anglers sit on one spot all day thinking of the limit they once took from that weed bed four years ago that averaged five pounds apiece.

As you spend time on the water pre-fishing an area, I must stress the importance of keeping an open mind and a closed mouth to EVERYONE. While on the water you will run into other tournament fishermen all trying to get an edge on you by saying they have found the mother load and took twenty fish in the first hour. These games tournament anglers play on each other is part of the fun, but DO NOT let it influence you in any way! First time anglers are often in awe of bragging anglers who collect a crowd at the boat launch. No matter how strongly I warn people, it is human nature to become intimidated by what other anglers are saying. This often changes their own strategies to what the braggart was doing.

Doing your own thing is the only way you will ever win a tournament. Listening to gossip will only cloud your thinking and confuse the game plan you have worked hard to put together. Be your own man, develop your own areas and secrets for catching bass. Doing your own thing is listed as one of the major keys to your success as a tournament angler. Many fishermen have not yet developed their skills so they can fish on their own, and trial and error will soon show them that they simply cannot place high in tournaments by listening to gossip.

Only one person can win a contest, so you must develop a style of fishing that is right for you. Many may ask what style is right and what is wrong? The answer to that question is simply gauged by your success at the end of the day.

Your efforts by the end of the pre-fishing days should have yielded at least six different areas. Each of these areas should be able to produce at least one keeper-size fish. For two day competitions you should have at least twelve areas holding fish. This may sound like a lot, but I can bet you right now that your first three spots won't hold a fish, and you will be forced to pull out all the stops when competition begins. Being overly prepared is the least of your worries.

Developing a game plan is like a game of chess. Factors such as weather, lake size, time of day, number of contestants, and your position in the start can affect your day on the water.

To me, this part is the most fun but also holds the most suspense. You never stop wondering how many other fishermen already know your hot spot. Nothing must distract you from fishing areas you wish to fish, but the key here is designing sort of a milk run of spots to fish. You will never fish a tournament where you will be the first to fish every spot you would like. This is why, during the pre-fish period, you take the time to learn the area a little better than the average guy so you will be able to take fish from an area that has been fished before.

Bass often work one area in the morning and slip to different areas for the majority of the day. Tournament anglers call these areas simply morning spots or late spots. Often in individual competition, two anglers might flip a coin to earn rights to fish a favorite morning spot first. It works out great when one angler has a morning spot while the other has a late spot. This way the two will not even need to flip a coin.

Obviously, it is best to have your entire day planned out beforehand. As the day progresses, adjust your plan to be the most productive. Going for boat rides is not my idea of fishing. Try to arrange your day so that you spend very little time running from spot to spot.

One very common question I get asked is how long do I stay in one spot before moving. First off, I never use a time table in covering the areas I wish to fish. Each spot must be fished completely and only when the fish seem to shut off will I head to my new area.

Again, we must reflect on the importance of learning the areas during the pre-fish period. You should have some idea of how long it will take to fish an area from past experience, and have a very good idea of where to start and stop your fishing activities.

Common courtesy is very important if you wish to fish this type of competition on a regular basis. Other anglers will be quick to label you a "meat hawg" if you keep the

Avid bass anglers are often all smiles when a dandy largemouth like this is taken during competition. It is every bass angler's dream to catch a limit of big bass in competition. With hard work and lots of practice, tournament fishing can be very rewarding.

front end of the boat towards the fishing areas with no regard for the guy in the back. You should never pull in front of another boat. This is true even if they are fishing YOUR favorite hot spot. It is best to go around the area you wish to fish, even if you feel there is no other area then work back towards the other boat.

Many tournaments have the basic courtesy rule of not fishing within 50 yards of an anchored boat or one which has thrown a marker to pin-point the area they call their own. A violation of this 50-yard rule could result in disqualification.

It is always nice to start each tournament on your #1 spot, but it is often more practical to fish other areas on the way to your honey-hole unless you have a fast enough boat to guarantee reaching your spot first. Fast boats are nice, but in nine out of ten tournaments, speed is not a reason or an excuse for catching more fish. In fact, many of the big pro's down south fish the large reservoirs with small boats instead of the big rockets and they do very well.

Mind games are played to the fullest just before a tournament begins. You must not be suckered into changing your game plan one bit. You must win the contest fishing your spots, with your methods, and with your style. Only then will you be able to place in competition on a consistent basis.

Once you begin to fish, stay loose and alert at all times. Just because you don't score on the first spot is no reason to give up and loose your concentration. What separates the good fishermen from the great fishermen is the level of concentration they maintain all day long. If you are not strong enough to cast all day long without taking a break, you will have problems. If you must stop for a coffee break or cigarette break, then you will have problems. Keeping your mind on the fish and not on the competition is the name of the game. You need to catch one bass at a time, and that is the only thing that should be on your mind.

The milk run, as I call it, is often a circular path around a lake that starts and ends close to the tournament headquarters. My way of tournament fishing is different from others who would rather sink or swim in one spot all day long. I am never more than a five minute boat ride from one spot to another. Your day should be spent fishing and not riding from spot to spot. This is especially true if you are fishing from a smaller boat and wish to do well. All the fishermen may be going to the other side of the lake to find fish, but it could take a half hour of valuable fishing time to get there with a small boat. Your pre-fishing time should have been spent finding areas near the tournament headquarters to maximize the time you have to fish.

In team competition, I feel it is good to communicate with your partner at all times. But one thing should be clear right from the very start.There must be a captain! Two excellent individuals very seldom fish well as a team because each has developed his own style of fishing. With one person fishing and the other making the decisions, the team can fish with more confidence. My tournament fishing partner and I have been fishing together for a long time. After so many years, I can almost tell you what my partner is thinking before he says it. When we fish together for money, I call the shots and he concentrates on only catching fish. Our styles of fishing are nearly the same, but if we both struggled to tell the other where to fish the team concept would fall apart.

With individual competition, you first must beat the person in your boat if you hope to win the contest. One of the first things to get straight is which boat to use and who will get the first four hours of running the boat. If there is any doubt as to how this should be done, flip a coin.

At no point should you feel obligated to describe why you are fishing in a particular spot during your time at the controls. Many tournament anglers try not to be harsh or snobbish, but they have spent many hours looking for their spots and to share what they have learned with a total stranger would be asking a lot. Some openly share their spots, while others don't say a word all day long. You can be sure of only one thing, expect the unexpected.

One of the tricks to fishing against the person who is running the boat is to keep your lure near his. Always wait for him to cast and place your cast just a little farther away. Keep an eye on what he is using and how he is using it.

There is one very important rule to remember when faced with a situation where your partner is catching fish while you can't seem to get a lick. This is especially true if he is using a lure you do not have. Don't try to fish like him! He may be an expert at crankbait fishing while you may not even own one. The day of the contest is too late to learn a new style of fishing. Many skilled anglers can effectively switch from one style to another and be equally productive, but only time and practice can build this kind of confidence.

Doing your own thing pays off big, but it may not seem that way if your partner has you down by four fish. Stick to your guns and work hard until it is your time to run the boat, because he will surely ease up and get sloppy. A good mental attitude and concentration is the key to success when you need to come from behind to win. Never give up. Never think for a moment that you're done for the day just because your partner has his limit and you still have a skunk in the box.

Work only areas where you found fish during the pre-fish days when time gets short. At all times you will need to maximize the odds of putting a fish in the boat. Of course, you NEVER want to fish new water at any time during the tournament.

By the end of the pre-fish period and the one or two days of competition, you should be physically worn out and ready to sleep for a week! Fishing fifteen hours a day in practice and the pressure and excitement of competition is a real drain on the human body. Keeping in good physical condition, as with any sport, makes you a better contestant. Anyone who says that fishing isn't work has never felt the draining emotional pressure of tournament fishing.

Any angler who is interested in bass fishing but is not interested in fishing for blood and big bucks might like getting involved with one of the many B.A.S.S Federations located in his state. These bass anglers form small clubs who travel to local lakes for small club tournaments. These smaller scale tournaments can give you the confidence to fish some of the big money contests in your area. You can find out more about the B.A.S.S. organizations in your state by contacting: Bass Anglers Sportsman Society, 1 Bell Road, Montgomery, AL 36141

CHAPTER ELEVEN
Fishing a New Lake

Truly one of the biggest challenges that could confront a fisherman is starting to fish on a few lake. Here in the North Country, we are blessed with thousands of natural lakes. Every one of these lakes is different from the next in some way. Understanding how bass can be found in these lakes doesn't have to be a nightmare.

One of the best parts of my job as an outdoor writer is that I get to fish many different lakes every year. Some people may dread the thought of fishing a new lake, I get all excited. Fishing a new lake is a new challenge and a learning experience. It is probably the reason I have kept such a high interest in fishing for all these years. I simply never grow tired of exploring new waters and discovering what a lake may offer.

Every lure and method of fishing we have talked about could be called into use at any time. The real secret to being successful on new waters is to be a well rounded bass angler first. Time and time again you will be relying on past experiences to help you uncover the mysteries of a new lake.

Once a new lake has been selected to fish you will need some type of map of the lake. It is very important that you know how the lake is shaped and any of the obvious bottom contours. Many of the lake maps available today are just a rough estimate of what you will find below. Never put too much importance on the exact depths they point out. It is far more critical to note where the steep and gradual breaks may be found.

If lake maps are not available, you will need to take your boat on a little tour of the lake. With your depth finder running at all times, you should make a circle around the entire lake. If you encounter any unique points or islands take the time to learn their size, shape, and distance from shore. Some fishermen may be able to memorize what they have learned from their boat ride, while others find it helpful to make some notes.

Once a basic understanding of the lake shape is known, it is important that you learn where the weed beds are located and how deep the weedline grows in that particular lake. This is especially true if you are out after largemouth. Smallmouth anglers need to take special note of shoreline

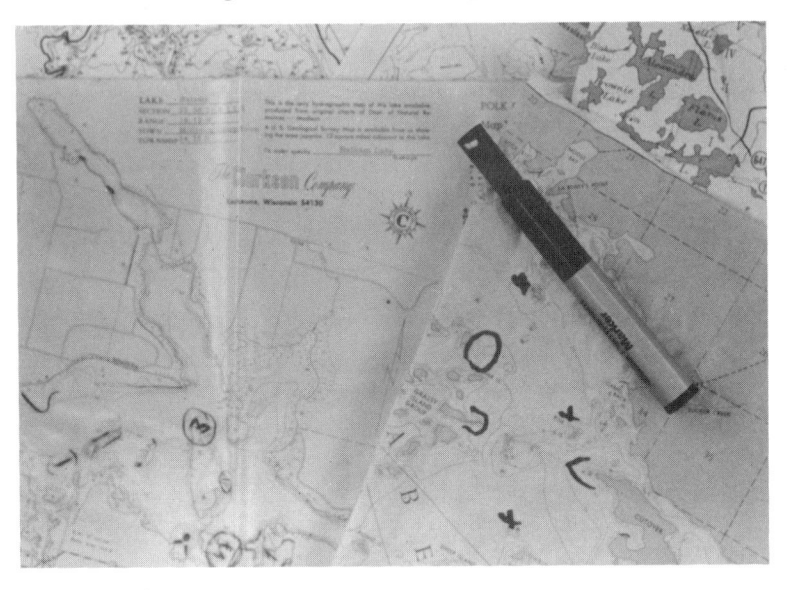

Lake maps aid the angler in many ways. Be sure to mark any "hotspot" for future reference and record any special things that may be of interest on another trip.

content. Boulders along a stretch of shoreline could mean boulders in deeper water as well.

The actual fishing procedures you must follow in a new lake consist of these major points.

1. Always start fishing familiar shoreline spots first. Simply fishing the shoreline will give you a chance to better understand what the lake is like. If, in your travels around the lake, you see something that resembles a productive spot you have fished in the past, then start there.

2. Never stop the boat while you are fishing. This rule will force you to cover a lot of water and learn more about

these new waters. Fishing one small area all day, just because you caught a few bass, will not teach you anything new about what the lake has to offer.

3. Have several rods rigged and ready for action at all times. This will make it possible to try different methods and techniques of fishing these strange bass until you find some that work. More than once I have stumbled upon situations where the bass wouldn't touch a spinnerbait, but they went crazy over crankbaits. By keeping several rods rigged and ready for action, you will be able to try new lures at any time.

4. Only AFTER fishing the shallow waters should you move deeper. This is a very important rule, because the odds are much greater of you finding an aggressive school of bass in shallow water than in deep. Granted, there may be some outstanding catches to be made in deep water. Deep water fishing means that you must fish slower, and unless you are in the right spot to start with, you could be skunked.

5. Ask for help wherever you can find it. Even though you are a topnotch bass fisherman, keep an open mind. More than once the casual bobber fisherman has been kind enough to put me on bass and not even know it. There is nothing wrong with taking some time to chat with the locals or other fishermen.

These five steps to fishing a new lake make it possible for you to head for new waters. These time-saving tips will put you on bass in a very short period of time. If there was one final thing I could tell you, it would be to stay flexible and keep an open mind. The most successful anglers in the country are those who are willing to keep learning.

CHAPTER TWELVE

FLY FISHING FOR BASS

Many of us can remember those fishing shows where Curt Gowdy was on a Colorado trout stream with a fly rod. It seemed as if he could cast a hundred yards. The skill he must have to control so much line is what actually got me into fly fishing. The almost magical way a fly line could be controlled by a skilled angler left me in complete awe.

It seems that in the bass fishing world, you are either a fly fisherman or you are not. Far too many people push aside fishing bass with a fly rod, thinking that it takes too much practice. This has changed a great deal in recent

Fly fishing for bass is a sport that more and more anglers are starting to experience. This fine stringer of smallmouth came on one small popper. The way these fish fight is something to see! Maybe you should try a little fly fishing this season.

years. This is why I have decided to write about fly fishing in this book. In years past, the fly fisherman was one who spent big bucks on specialized tackle and this tackle needed special care. It had earned a reputation as being a rich man's sport. This reputation is another factor that is keeping it from the average angler who feels that he could never master this aspect of fishing. No longer are fly rods for trout fishing only! Anglers, more than ever, are finding new and exciting ways to enjoy the their sport.

I haven't seen a book yet that can do justice to the teaching of fly rod casting. Everyone seems to have different problems when they get started. Being able to spot your own problems and correcting them is almost impossible. For this reason, I would like anyone who wishes to learn to cast a fly rod to simply ask someone to show you. You may get help from a local fly fishing club, or maybe from a local tackle shop.

It really only takes a few minutes under experienced supervision to get the hang of working a fly rod. I can remember the times when I would stop traffic in downtown Minneapolis to show a customer how to work his new fly rod. The basic stroke of picking the line up off the water and laying it back down is all you need to get started. Casting distance is of little importance in fly fishing. One of the biggest problems I have found with anglers is that they want to cast farther than their skills will permit. Line control comes first, casting distance is a far second.

Fly Fishing Equipment

By far one of the biggest advantages in modern technology is the new materials that have made fly fishing so simple and maintenance free. There is even a rating system for matching fly rods to fly lines aiding in making the proper selection of equipment.

Fly rods come in many different materials. The price you will pay often reflects the total weight of the rod and its ability to cast longer distances. Materials such as graphite and boron have made a big difference to fly fishermen. The first graphite rods were actually designed for the fly fishermen. The basic problem with big water rods is that they were too heavy to handle for long periods of time and they lost control of heavier lines at great distances.

Someone getting into fly fishing need not go overboard and spend a fortune on gear. A good starting fly rod for bass fishing will run about thirty dollars. For bass fishing, the fly rod should be no shorter than eight feet in length.

In fly fishing, you must always remember that you are casting the weight of the line and not the lure. This concept is the key to your ability to control the line at longer distances. Your rod must be balanced with the right line weight otherwise it becomes difficult to cast. There is a recommended line rating on the shaft of every fly rod sold today. I prefer to use a rod rated for a #8 or #9 fly line.

There are many different types of fly lines on the market to choose from, and this is an area where anglers may get confused. The rating system for lines is now standard for every manufacturer, so it is easier to match the proper line to your needs. On a spool of line you will find the code DT (double taper), WF (weight forward taper) or L (level taper) in front of a number followed by an S (sinking) or a F (floating). On a spool it would read like this, WF8F. This means that the line has a weight forward taper with a number 8 rating to the line and the F stands for floating.

A taper is given to a fly line to give the fisherman different options in performance. A "DT" (double taper) line is often used by trout fishermen who fish at short range. The line is actually tapered for use on both ends. When a fisherman wears out one portion of line after a few years, he can just unwind the line and re-wind it backwards to use the other side of the taper. This is a money saving feature for those who like to fish a lot and never need to cast great distances. Once you realize a need to cast over 40 feet, "WF" (weight forward) line can be used. This line has only one taper for better casting distance. The "L" (level) line is simply a length of line without a taper to it at all. These lines are often good to practice with and are the least expensive. A tapered line can easily cost twenty-five dollars per roll, where a level line may only cost five dollars. The tapered lines make for a much better casting action and the bass bug tends to land on the water more gracefully.

In fly fishing, the lines are not rated in a pound test, but by how much the first thirty feet of line weighs. A #4 line is very light and is used for trout fishing. The #6 rating is considered the average line and is the biggest seller for trout and panfish anglers. A larger line size is needed to carry out a larger, more air resistant bass bug. For this type of fishing, a #8 or #9 line is commonly used. If, for some reason, you need to reach out great distances, a #10 line on a rod designed to handle a line of this weight would carry out the largest of bass bugs and poppers even in the wind.

Floating fly lines will make up about 99% of your fishing needs for bass. Once you do more fly fishing, you may wish to try using streamers that run below the surface. This is the time to use an "S" or sinking line.

A short leader must be added to the end of the fly line. This leader need not be anything too fancy for bass fishing as compared to trout fishing. In trout fishing, even the slightest ripple on the water could result in spooking a fish. Trout anglers may use leaders up to twelve feet long. They will taper from twenty-pound test on one end, to only one-pound test where the fly is attached. Tapered leaders are really not needed in bass fishing, but some anglers still like to use them. I only use a six foot length of twelve-pound test line for the entire leader. It is important that you use a fairly stiff line to make the bass bug roll out to the end of your cast. A common problem when using a tapered leader with too fine of a tip section is that your bug ends up in a pile of fishing line. Unless the line is stiff enough to keep the bait turning over, you will have a problem of the bug loosing power before it reaches its maximum distance. The larger the bug, the stiffer the leader you must use in order to make it land properly on the water.

    The reel you select to mount on your fly rod is of little importance in your ability to cast or even to fight a fish. Many people think that you fight a fish with a fly reel like you might with a conventional reel, but actually you are hand-lining each fish and the reel doesn't play a part in the action. The reel is simply a place to hold line. You need not spend an arm and a leg for a fly reel. Twenty dollars for a single-action fly reel is more than enough, but make sure that it is large enough to handle the line size you will fish.

Fly Fishing Lures

    The family of bass bugs are basically geared to topwater lures, but many anglers use streamers and large nymph patterns with great success. For anyone just getting into the sport, I highly recommend staying with topwater lures. They will enable you to learn line control and how to work different lures with a fly rod. Fishing sub-surface lures will demand great amounts of line control and this will come with time.

    The hard balsa wood poppers have long been a traditional lure for bass fishermen. The size of the popper that you select should have a lot to do with the weather conditions, and not the size of fish you wish to catch. On windy days, a large bass bug is very difficult to control. For this reason, a smaller bug is a wise selection.

    There are a series of bass bugs that are made completely out of deer hair. These types of bugs really grab the air when they are cast. Only the longest and most powerful rods can handle these bugs with any accuracy. I personally prefer to fish the hard body poppers in contrast to the deer hair bugs for just this reason.

The shape of a popper will enable you to give a different action to the way it is retrieved. Some bass bugs have a blunt nose for pushing water, and others have a depressed nose for making a popping sound as they are pulled through the water. Bass bugs are designed to be fished with your rod tip pointed towards the water. The fly line is held with a single finger of the same hand that holds the rod. Your other hand grabs the line that hangs under the handle. With your free hand you apply a series of short pulls or long sweeps. Some poppers, like those with pointed noses, will actually dive below the surface with just one pull of the

Poppers and streamer flies come in many different shapes. The size of the popper or bug you are throwing should be matched to a rod strong enough to cast the lure into the wind. Although these baits are small in size, they can attract some very large bass.

line. It is critical that the rod itself is not used to give action to the popper. Your rod must always remain in the perfect position to take up the slack and set the hooks quickly.

As with fishing any topwater lure, you must spot and fish around shallow forms of "visible structure". With practice, you will be surprised at just how accurate you can be with a fly rod. When a strike occurs, it is again impor-

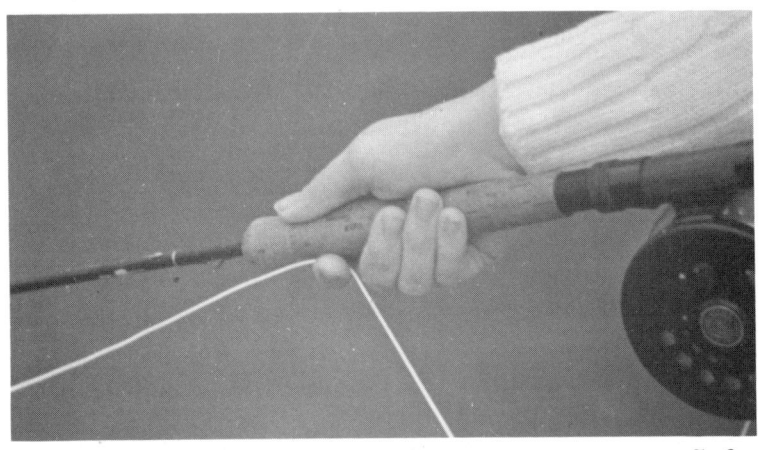

Good line control is critical to working a popper or streamer fly for bass. The line must run through one finger, and the line is pulled and controlled with the other hand. This makes it possible to have control of the line at all times. Remember to keep your rod tip pointed downwards and to work the line, not the rod, to give action to your bass bugs and flies.

tant NOT to set the hooks when the strike is seen. The boil you see is the bass coming up to grab the bait. In fly fishing, it seems even more critical to keep an eye on your popper at all times. The largest fish will often barely ripple the water as they take your bait. Be sure to really lift up hard on the rod to set the hooks. The real key to bass fishing with a popper is to not be in a hurry to set the hooks. In my opinion, you can never set the hooks too late after a strike.

Fly fishing for bass is one of the most exciting and rewarding ways to fish. Over the next few years I am sure more people will be aware of just how much fun bass fishing with a long rod can be. It will take only one trip with a person who knows how to handle a fly rod to convince you that there is more than one way to catch a bass.

CHAPTER THIRTEEN

LIVE BAIT FISHING FOR BASS

There is no doubt about the effectiveness of live bait on bass here in the North Country. Largemouth and smallmouth bass will grab many different types of offerings. You have the traditional baits such as minnows, night crawlers, and of course frogs. Then there are the little known baits like crayfish, salamanders and hellgrammites.

The reason for only mentioning live bait in this special section is that most avid bass anglers frown on the use of live bait. This does not mean that anglers who use live bait are cheating. Far from it! It takes a great amount of angling skill to work with live bait. The big difference is that bass simply have a hard time turning down live bait. Even when weather conditions are not favorable, live bait fishermen can really do a job on bass. The major reason that some anglers turn their noses up at those who fish live bait is that live bait is NOT permitted in many of the money tournaments. Many purists feel that a true bass fisherman would never stoop to fishing live bait.

Time and time again I have worked over an area with artificials only to have a boat pull in behind me and take some nice bass using live bait. No one will argue that at times the bass is one critter who can be very finicky. If these occasions arise, then why not use live bait to help things along?

There are many different ways live bait can be fished. I like to work with only the most popular, and the ones which I have found to be effective in our northern waters. For example, one of the deadliest lure and live bait combinations is the jig and minnow. Smallmouth, in particular, are real suckers for this. This is the same jig and minnow combination used by walleye fishermen. The minnow can

The jig and minnow combination is tough to beat for smallmouth fishing in deep water. Take special note of how the minnow is added to the hook for best results. This is one of my personal fishing secrets that can mean more fish for you as well.

be added to a plain jig head or to a more fancy jig with feathers or rubber for the body.

The old reliable Lindy Rig concept, which is just a hook with a piece of line and a sinker, is all the angler may need. Often referred to as a live bait rig, the Lindy Rig can be fished with a minnow, night crawler, frog, or even a ribbon leech, and will do very well on both species of bass.

With any form of live bait, we must realize the importance of fishing the bait on or near the bottom. In some areas "the bottom" may mean fishing over the tops of the weeds. This means that your tackle must be balanced to match conditions for its best performance. For example, the smallmouth may be running deep in a clear lake as winter approaches. The use of a jig and minnow combination is by far your #1 choice. If you are to be fishing in waters of twenty-five feet, it is wise to use a jig of at least 3/8 ounce to reach the bottom. The next chart gives the recommended jig size for the depths you will be fishing. If, for some reason, you simply can't feel the bottom, then keep switching to a heavier jig until you are in contact with the bottom at all times.

1/8 ounce	two to six feet
1/4 ounce	six to twelve feet
1/2 ounce	twelve to twenty feet
3/4 ounce	twenty to thirty-two feet
1 ounce	thirty-two to forty-five feet

Hook size is another very important factor when you are working with live bait. First, we already know that bass don't nibble a bait, they gulp it down. This means that you have no excuse to not use a larger hook with your live bait. Fishing with a live frog is a good example of a need to use a large hook. A large, tasty frog, when grabbed by a bass, could make it very difficult for a small hook to find the jaw of the bass. The frog can easily be rolled in the mouth of the bass making it almost impossible to set the hooks. For this type of fishing I recommend at least a #1/0 hook size with a short shaft. The chart below lists the most popular baits and the corresponding hook sizes that should be used for best success.

Minnows
#2 or #4 hook (fathead and small chubs)

Leeches
#4 hook (only black ribbon leech)

Frogs
#1/0 hook (this number will vary slightly with size)

Salamanders
#2/0 hook (adults)

Waterdogs
#1/0 hook (immature salamanders)

Night crawlers
#4 hook

Crayfish
#2 hook (soft shell type is best)

This gives us at least a starting point for hook size when we use a live bait rig setup. The other critical factor with a live bait rig is the sinkers used to keep the bait down where the fish are.

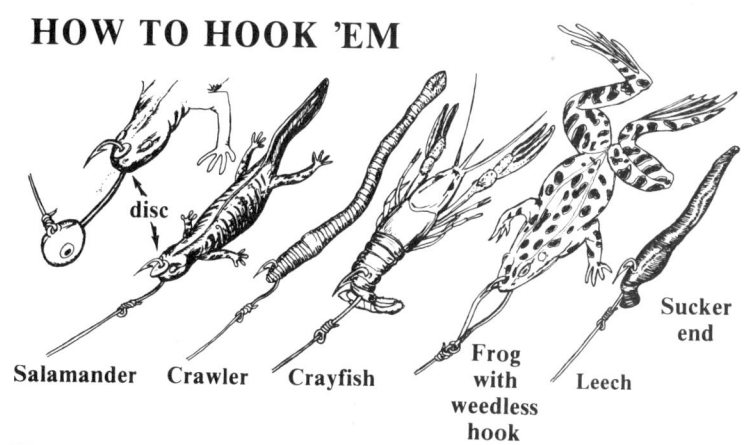

HOW TO HOOK 'EM

Salamander — disc | Crawler | Crayfish | Frog with weedless hook | Leech | Sucker end

The above diagram shows the various ways to hook live bait. Wire leaders and heavy snap-swivels should be avoided at all costs to make your bait offering as attractive as possible.

The actual locations where you fish live bait are not all that different from those I have already described. The major difference is that you will end up fishing live bait slower than artificials. The use of a bobber is not at all out of line when you are working over the tops of heavy weeds or snags.

Setting the hooks with live bait does not have to mean gut-hooking the bass. Obviously, it is easy to just feed out line and let the fish swallow the bait, but this is unnecessary. Just as with artificials, the bass will gulp the bait down in the blink of an eye. The only critical factor to your success is the angle that you have on the bass when you set the hooks. To increase your odds, wait only long enough for the bass to be swimming away from you before you strike. Don't be sheepish in you hook-set either. When live bait fishing, you often have much more slack line in the water than you'd think. You try to set the hooks, and you end up just pulling up the slack line.

Spring smallmouth often hold deeper than the largemouth. Because of this, the jig and minnow combination is a top choice for early season smallmouth anglers. As you can see, many of the largest fish of the year will be taken at this time.

If, by chance, the bass is gut hooked, don't take any chances of the bass dying. It is a far better idea to simply cut your line just above the hook. By doing this, you will not damage the bass. In a week or so, the acids in the mouth or stomach will dissolve the hook with no pain to the bass.

The use of live bait is a wise idea during the cold months of the year. When bass activity is slow, live bait seems to be the ticket to consistent success. Live bait is often the only way to go after a cold front comes through. Some days it seems like someone turned off a switch. On these days live bait might be the only way to take bass.

Of the baits I have talked about so far, one I'm sure, is new to many. Salamanders are an extremely effective bass bait if you can get them. Although I have taken both large and small bass on them, they are considered a big fish bait. The salamander is like a frog in that immature salamanders live under the water, and as they grow they develop legs and move onto land. An immature salamander is called a waterdog.

If you have a good bait dealer in your town, you might have him order you some of these effective bass baits. I've fished with salamanders and waterdogs for the past five years since they became popular. All I read and heard was that these new baits were an unfair advantage. Big bass just couldn't resist them! The cost for these critters can run up to two dollars apiece, and for that they had better work miracles! I have been disappointed by their performance so far, and although I have taken several nice fish on them, the old reliable frog has been much more practical.

Leeches have proven to be very effective on smallmouth bass. Many a walleye fisherman gets his first taste of smallmouth fishing as one of these scrappy fish tears up his tackle. The ribbon leech is the preferred bait for smallmouth, not the large, spotted horse leech we find in our lakes. Although I have taken several bass with leeches in their stomachs, I have never hooked a bass on one. The ribbon leech is a swamp leech and runs in color from a dark brown to black. Leeches can be fished on a plain hook or dressed on a jig with good success. Leeches are just plain great on smallmouth, and largemouth have a hard time turning them down as well.

Night crawlers have long been one of the favorite baits of bass fishermen. These, also, can be used on a plain hook or dressed on a jig. Smallmouth and largemouth bass alike love a fat, juicy night crawler. Keeping this bait fresh is the secret to better catches. Crawlers should be kept cool or cold at all times for best results. Nothing is worse than a rotten night crawler for catching bass. Most anglers keep their crawlers in small coolers packed with ice to prevent the sun from cooking them.

The minnows used for bass fishing can range from four inch suckers to tiny crappie minnows added to the backs of jigs. In Florida, large shiners are considered to be the top choice for a big fish bait. I must have seen two dozen fishing shows where anglers were fishing with shiners and catching ten pound bass. Will this technique work up in our North Country for bass? You bet! Large shiners and suckers have produced some of the largest bass of my lifetime.

Shiners seem to be more effective than suckers for this type of fishing, but finding large shiners is tough. You can imagine that you will run into a few northern pike, walleye, and even muskie fishing these large shiners. And that can be fun too! These big minnows are often six inches long, but they are rigged just as if you were crappie fishing. The bobber, sinkers, and hooks are larger of course, but the same basic rig is used. Smaller minnows such as the fathead and redtail chub are best used with a jig, especially a plain jig head if the minnow is over two inches long.

On Lake Erie, crayfish is one of the most effective baits you could use on smallmouth bass. The crayfish is particularly effective just after it sheds a layer of hard shell.

Minnow buckets come in all different shapes and designs. During the colder months of the year, a foam bucket will do a fine job of keeping the minnows alive, but during the summer, a bucket that can be submerged into the water is a easier way of getting fresh water to the minnows. The warmer the water, the more oxygen their bodies will demand.

They are referred to as a "soft shell cray". These are the crayfish in the highest demand for smallmouth fishing. Most of the good smallmouth fishing is in September and October, so the crayfish need to be shipped in from down south. They might cost thirty cents or more apiece when the demand is up and the supply is low.

The transportation of crayfish from one lake to another is prohibited in some states. Be sure to check your laws about the transportation of any form of bait. Back in the midwest the use of crayfish is something that has yet to catch on, and for that reason many bait dealers will not stock these critters. The only times I have used crayfish in my home state of Minnesota have been when I have to go out to catch a few myself, then head out fishing. The results have always been good, and I am sure that more and more bait fishermen will be taking advantage of this great form of bait in the future.

There are, of course, many more forms of live bait that anglers could use to catch bass. Grubs, earth worms, crickets, grass hoppers, hellgrammites, toads, and even field mice have been used to catch bass. Live bait is by far a more consistent way to score on bass when compared to the use of artificial lures. But live bait fishermen still must be able to put the bait in the right spot to be successful.

STATE RECORD BASS CATCHES

State	Weight (Pounds - Ounces)	Angler	Location	Year
Alabama	(Lm)14-8½	Andy J. Stewart	Public Lake	1983
	(Sm)10-8	Owen F. Smith	Wheeler Dam	1950
Arizona	(Lm)14-2	Ed Smith	Roosevelt Lake	1956
	(Sm) 6-14	Joseph A. Cross	Roosevelt Lake	1980
Arkansas	(Lm)16-4	Johnny Manning	Lake DeGray	1983
	(Sm) 7-5	Acie Dickerson	Bull Shoals	1969
California	(Lm)21-3	Raymond Easley	Lake Casitas	1980
	(Sm) 9-1	Tim Brady	Clair Engle Lake	1976
Colorado	(Lm)10-6	Sharon Brunson	Stalker Lake	1979
	(Sm) 5-5	Russ Moran	Smith Reservoir	1979
Connecticut	(Lm)12-14	Frank Domurat	Mashapaug Lake	1961
	(Sm) 7-12	Jos. Mankauskas, Jr.	Shenipsit Lake	1980
Delaware	(Lm)10-5	Tony Kaczmarczyk	Andrews Lake	1980
	(Sm) 4-7	Richard Williams	—	1983
Florida	(Lm)19-0	W.A. Witt	Lake Tarpon	1961
Georgia	(Lm)22-4	George Perry	Montgomery Lake	1932
	(Sm) 7-2	Jack Hill	Lake Chatuge	1973
Hawaii	(Lm) 8-0	Earl Vito	Kilauea, Kauai	1978
	(Sm) 3-11	Willie Song	Lake Wilson	1982

STATE RECORD BASS CATCHES

State	Weight (Pounds - Ounces)	Angler	Location	Year
Idaho	(Lm) 10-15	Mrs. M.W. Taylor	Anderson Lake	—
	(Sm) 7-5	Don B. Schiefelbein	Dworshak Res.	1982
Illinois	(Lm) 13-1	Edward J. Walbel	Stone Quarry Lake	1976
	(Sm) 6-5	Gene Wyatt	Farm Pond	1980
Indiana	(Lm) 11-11	Curt Reynolds	Ferdinand Res.	1968
	(Sm) 6-8	Jim Connerly	Stream	1970
Iowa	(Lm) 10-12	Patricia Zaerr	Lake Fisher	1984
	(Sm) 6-8	Rick Pentland	Spirit Lake	1979
Kansas	(Lm) 11-12	Ken Bingham	Farm Pond	1977
	(Sm) 4-11	Terry Stanton	Milford Res.	1983
Kentucky	(Lm) 13-8	Delbert Grizzle	Greenbo Lake	1966
	(Sm) 11-15	David Hayes	Dale Hollow Lake	1955
Louisiana	(Lm) 12-0	Harold Dunaway	Farm Pond	1975
Maine	(Lm) 11-10	Robert Kamp	Moose Pond	1968
	(Sm) 8-0	George Dyer	Thompson Lake	1970
Maryland	(Lm) 11-2	Rodney Cockrell	Farm Pond	1983
	(Sm) 8-4	Gary Peters	Liberty Res.	1974
Massachusetts	(Lm) 15-8	Walter Bolonis	Sampson's Pond	1975
	(Sm) 7-0	Marshall Hunter	Lovell's Pond	1972

State			Angler	Location	Year
Michigan	(Lm)	11-15	Wm. Maloney	Big Pine Is. Lake	1934
		11-15	Jack Rorex	Bamfield Dam	1959
Minnesota	(Sm)	9-4	W.F. Shoemaker	Long Lake	1906
	(Lm)	9-4	Fritz Schneider	Washington Lake	1978
Mississippi	(Sm)	8-0	John Creighton	West Battle Lake	1948
	(Lm)	13-8	Lucious Gregory	Farm Pond	1974
	(Sm)	7-5	Jesse Clifton	Pickwick Res.	1976
Missouri	(Lm)	13-14	Marvin Bushong	Bull Shoals	1961
	(Sm)	6-12	Dr. Norman Klayman	Bull Shoals	1983
Montana	(Lm)	7-8	Bruce Blahnik	Kicking Horse Res.	1980
	(Sm)	4-11	Bob Higson	Horseshoe Lake	1975
Nebraska	(Lm)	10-11	Paul Abegglen	Sandpit	1965
	(Sm)	6-1	Walley Allison	Merritt Res.	1978
Nevada	(Lm)	11-0	H.P. Warner	Lake Mohave	1972
	(Sm)	2-15	Charles Smith	Lahontan Res.	1981
New Hampshire	(Lm)	10-8	G. Bullpitt	Lake Potanipo	1967
	(Sm)	7-14	Francis Lord	Goose Pond	1970
New Jersey	(Lm)	10-14	Robert Eisele	Menantico Pond	1980
	(Sm)	6-4	Earl Trumpore	Delaware River	1957
New Mexico	(Lm)	11-0	Bud Marks	Ute Lake	1975
	(Sm)	6-8	Carl Kelly	Ute Lake	1972

STATE RECORD BASS CATCHES

State	Weight (Pounds - Ounces)	Angler	Location	Year
New York	(Lm) 10-12	Matthew Rutkowski	Chadwick Lake	1975
	(Sm) 9-0	George Tennyson	Friends Lake	1925
North Carolina	(Lm) 14-15	Leonard Williams	Santeetlah Res.	1963
	(Sm) 10-2	Archie Lampkin	Hiwassee Res.	1953
North Dakota	(Lm) 8-7	Leon Rixen	Nelson Lake	1983
	(Sm) 5-0	M. Erhart	Sakakawea	1982
Ohio	(Lm) 13-2	Roy Landsberger	Farm Pond	1976
	(Sm) 7-8	James Bayless	Mad River	1941
Oklahoma	(Lm) 12-1	James Porter	Lake Lawtonka	1983
	(Sm) 5-10	Charles Love	Broken Bow	1983
Oregon	(Lm) 10-15	Butch Stauffacher	Selmac Lake	1983
	(Sm) 6-13	Mark Weir	Brownlee Res.	1978
Pennsylvania	(Lm) 11-3	Don Shade	Birch Run Res.	1983
	(Sm) 7-4	Larry Ashbaugh	Youghiogheny River	1983
Rhode Island	(Lm) 10-0	Ray LeBlanc	Abbott Run	1981
	(Sm) 5-15	Butch Ferris	Wash Pond	1977
South Carolina	(Lm) 16-2	Paul Flanagan	Lake Marion	1949
	(Sm) 5-4	Carl Hood	Toxaway River	1971

State		Size	Angler	Location	Year
South Dakota	(Lm)	8-12	Verne Page	Hayes Lake	1957
	(Sm)	8-12	Roger Kowell	Fraiser Lake	1974
Tennessee		4-6	Virgil McKee	Ft. Randall	1982
	(Lm)	14-8	Louge Barnett	Sugar Creek	1954
	(Sm)	11-15	D.L. Hayes	Dale Hollow Res.	1955
Texas	(Lm)	15-8	John Alexander	Echo Lake	1981
	(Sm)	6-2	David Vorak	Canyon Res.	1982
Utah	(Lm)	10-2	Sam LaManna	Lake Powell	1974
	(Sm)	6-12	Roger Tallerico	Lake Borham	1983
Vermont	(Lm)	8-4	Michael Poulin	Lake Morey	1983
	(Sm)	6-12	George Carlson	Lake Champlain	1978
Virginia	(Lm)	14-2	Bobby Creel	Gaston Lake	1975
	(Sm)	8-0	C.A. Garay	Claytor Lake	1964
Washington	(Lm)	11-9	—	Banks Lake	1977
	(Sm)	8-12	Ray Wanacutt	Columbia River	1967
West Virginia	(Lm)	10-13	William Wilhelm	Sleepy Creek L.	1979
	(Sm)	9-12	David Lindsay	South Branch	1971
Wisconsin	(Lm)	11-3	Robert Miklowski	Lake Ripley	1940
	(Sm)	9-1	Leon Stefoneck	Indian Lake	1950
Wyoming	(Lm)	7-2	John Teeters	Stove Lake	1942
	(Sm)	4-12	D. Jon Nelson	Slater Ash Creek	1982

215

WORLD RECORD BASS

Georgia	(Lm) 22-4	George Perry	Montgomery Lake	1932
Kentucky	(Sm) 11-15	David Hayes	Dale Hollow Lake	1955

THE FINEST BOOK SERIES IN PRINT!

Walleye Fishing Today, A true classic in every sense. This best selling book has become the cornerstone of modern walleye fishing strategies ANYWHERE in the country. Special sections include: Night fishing, fishing Lake Erie and the Missouri River system, tips to customize your fishing boat and much, much more. Don't miss this one!!

North Country Bassin', the *newest and finest* bass book ever written. This straight shooting manual of fishing secrets is geared for BOTH largemouth and smallmouth bass in Yankee Country. Special features include: Smallmouth in rivers, tournament strategies, dock fishing, lure selection and a lot more. A *must* for every bass angler.

Northern Pike! Solve the mysteries of catching big pike. This book has no equal if you are a pike lover. Up to date information and secrets never before put in print! Special sections include: Year round pike tactics, lure modifying, trolling tricks, deboning secrets and some great pike recipes.

ORDER TODAY!

Why not take the first step in becoming the very best you can be? Just send $9.95 for each book and add $1.00 for postage and handling (Minnesota residents add 6% sales tax) to. . .

Tom Zenanko Outdoors
5420 71st Circle North
Brooklyn Center, Minn. 55429